MW01533440

Copyright 2022 Dane Davis

All rights reserved. Small portions of this book may be used or reproduced for
personal use, sermons, small group Bible studies, or in the case of brief
quotations in critical articles and reviews.

All Scripture quotations are from the New International Version, 1984,
unless otherwise specified.

Lyrics to "God of This City" copyright © 2008 Thankyou Music (PRS) (adm.
worldwide at CapitolCMGPublishing.com excluding the UK & Europe which is
adm. at IntegratedRights.com) / worshiptogether.com Songs (ASCAP) sixsteps
Music (ASCAP) (adm. at CapitolCMGPublishing.com). All rights reserved.
Used by permission.

Lyrics to "Hosanna" copyright © 2007 Hillsong Music Publishing (APRA) (adm. in
the US and Canada at CapitolCMGPublishing.com). All rights reserved.
Used by permission.

Cover design and interior formatting by *Hannah Linder Designs*

The views expressed in this work are solely those of the author.

Hardcover: 9798846867826
Paperback: 9798351938776

DEDICATION

To Allan's amazing family and friends who have encouraged,
loved, inspired and prayed for him during his painful journey.

Perseverance doesn't happen in a vacuum.

CONTENTS

PART FIVE
10 DAYS TO PERSEVERE

A Medical Disclaimer

Within the following pages, several medical institutions and a few doctors are mentioned by name. In order to maintain accuracy, the author has chosen not to downplay Allan's negative experiences at some of these institutions or hide his disappointment with his doctors at times. Without exception, every physician who is mentioned by name worked hard to identify the root causes of Allan's pain and alleviate it. But none of these doctors were as successful as Allan had hoped, sometimes leaving him disappointed and frustrated.

Allan's disappointment and frustration are expressed in this book, but they are simply part of his story of coming to grips with an incurable disease. It is not intended to disparage any doctor or hospital. Quite the opposite: Both Allan and the author are deeply grateful for the many doctors in multiple institutions who fought for Allan's health. The fact is: Allan needed a miracle— something that no doctor or medical institution could realistically deliver. So, their efforts were bound to fail.

May this book remind us all that doctors and nurses do amazing work every day, but, often, their hands are tied and their power is limited. Ultimately, God is in control. In Allan's case, God chose to allow him to bear the burden of arachnoiditis, and there's nothing that any doctor or hospital could have done to alter God's plan.

So, in hindsight, Allan doesn't lay blame on anyone for his many treatments that *didn't* work. Doctors did their very best dealing with an impossible task, and for that we are all deeply grateful.

Introduction

"A friend loves at all times,
and a brother is born for adversity."
- Proverbs 17:17

In early March 2009, I received a call from a local mortuary in Victorville, California. A Christian family in our community had suffered a tragic loss. Their Uncle Ronnie had passed away, and they needed a pastor to officiate his funeral. Since I was on the mortuary's pastor-on-call list, they reached out to me. I was available, so on March 9, 2009, I donned my best gray suit, grabbed my Bible and headed to the memorial park to officiate a funeral service for a man I'd never met who was part of a family I didn't know.

I can't remember most of the details of what took place before, during or after the service. But there's one detail I'll never forget. After the service I met Uncle Ronnie's 20-year-old nephew, Allan Schwartz. Despite being in a wheelchair, dealing with a strange spinal cord disease I'd never heard of and suffering the loss of his uncle, Allan was a bundle of energy. Even in the minutes following his uncle's funeral, there was something strangely positive about him. His facial expressions were genuinely warm; his voice was enthusiastic, and he radiated an unexplainable joy. It seemed clear that Allan was one in a million.

In the months that followed, as Allan and his family began attending the church where I serve as pastor, I got to know Allan much better, and we quickly became friends. The more I learned about his amazing life story, the more I became convinced that God had a very special calling on his life—a calling that I was only beginning to understand.

Many excellent biographies have been written about men and women who have persevered through physical disabilities and traumatic injuries. Nick Vujicic, Joni Eareckson Tada and Bethany Hamilton come to mind. So, why write a biography about the young man with the funny last name who most people have never heard of? Two reasons: First, because Allan's story is extraordinary. And more importantly, because Allan's story of persevering through *his* trials has the potential to inspire countless others to persevere through *their* trials ... including you.

Allan's story of enduring a rare neurological disease is both captivating and life-changing. In the seventeen years since his crippling pain began, Allan has suffered through more doctors' visits, hospital stays, experimental treatments, misdiagnoses and surgeries than most people endure in a lifetime. And he has endured all of it with grit, determination and his trademark positive attitude.

Most remarkable of all is the fact that, through it all, Allan's faith in God has remained intact. It's *easy* to trust in God's goodness and power when we're on life's mountaintops with plenty of money in the bank, a happy marriage and a clean bill of health. It's much *harder* to believe in His goodness and power when our bank accounts are bled dry, our spouses walk out, and our prayers for healing remain unanswered.

So, you and I don't need to learn how to stand strong in our faith and persevere when our Christianity is *easy*. We need to learn how to stand strong in our faith and persevere when our Christianity is *hard*. And there are few people I know who can teach us how to do that better than Allan Schwartz. He doesn't just *talk* about trusting God through hard times, he has walked the walk for the past seventeen years. He doesn't just *preach* about persevering in our faith during times of testing, he is the *embodiment* of a Christ-follower who perseveres through unimaginable pain, disease and disappointment with God.

Jesus Christ has called Allan to persevere, and He has taught him how to do so. He has taught him many inspiring and life-changing lessons about faith and obedience—lessons that He desires to pass on to you as you read Allan's story.

So, I thank you for joining me as we open our minds and hearts to what the Lord has to teach us through Allan's amazing story. Allan has been called to persevere, and so have you.

Six-year-old Allan shows off his mullet and strikes his best
soccer pose for his AYSO team, the Hurricanes.

PART ONE

THE NEXT HALL OF FAMER

CHAPTER 1

SPORTS AND SCHOOL

*"There are different kinds of gifts, but the same Spirit.
There are different kinds of service, but the same Lord."*
- 1 Corinthians 12:4-5

A BUDDING SPORTS STAR

From the time he could walk, Allan was an Energizer bunny. He ran a mile a minute and "kept going and going and going." Nothing could stop him. Always on the go—especially when sports were involved. In the fall of 1991, at the age of three, Allan began playing organized team sports. He started with soccer, which he took to like a fish to water. He loved everything about it: the running, the jumping, the dribbling and especially the shooting and scoring. It was plain for any casual spectator to see: Allan was a very competitive little brown-haired bundle of energy.

Soccer was Allan's first love. He thought about it night and day and, if he had it his way, he would have slept with his soccer ball every night. So, you can imagine how traumatized he felt when his parents, Joe and Kim, broke the news to him: Soccer season only lasts a few months. Allan just couldn't wrap his mind around the horror of this unexpected turn of events.

But Allan's disappointment was short-lived, because in the off-season he discovered another sport that was almost as amazing as soccer ... baseball. Once Allan started playing it, he was hooked. If you handed him a bat and glove, he was ready. Anytime. Anywhere. Of all the team sports Allan would play during his childhood and teenage years, his first two sports, soccer and baseball, would always remain his favorites.

When Allan wasn't on the soccer field striving to be the next David Beckham or on the baseball mound mirroring Dodgers' hall-of-fame hitter Mike Piazza, he was usually playing in the neighborhood with his best friends Matt, Chris and Kevin. Their families had moved into a new Chino, California housing tract around the same time that Allan's family had. So, they grew up together and made sure there was never a dull moment. Allan and his buddies loved to shoot hoops, build forts, and ride their bikes and Razor scooters to the local AMPM to buy snacks. Safety wasn't a top priority for Allan. On more than one occasion he came home for dinner with scrapes up and down his shins and dried blood on his knees. Kim asked Allan why he hadn't come home right away after getting hurt. And in typical Allan fashion he answered, "It didn't hurt. I just wanted to keep playing!"

During summer vacation, when Allan and his friends weren't spilling their blood on the asphalt, they could often be found swimming in the Schwartzes' above ground pool. After long afternoons of cannonball contests and boy-powered whirlpools, it's a wonder that any water was still left in the pool at the end of the day. And it's an even bigger wonder that the Schwartzes' summer water bills didn't put Allan's parents in the poorhouse.

During those warm summer months, Kim liked to give the swimming pool a breather once or twice a week by taking Allan— along with his older brother Joey and younger sister Shavaun—to one of her favorite places on earth ... the beach. It was her "happy place." Kim felt so blessed to be able to load up her 1996 Chevy

Suburban and be at either Newport Beach or Huntington Beach in under forty-five minutes. And since there were four open seats in their red aircraft-carrier-on-wheels, there was always room for several of the kids' friends to join them for their sand-and-salt-water adventure. When Kim felt like hitting the waves, she took great pride in teaching Allan how to boogie board. And once he got the hang of it, he was a boogie boarding machine.

Holidays were when the families in Allan's neighborhood pulled out all the stops. When Easter, the Fourth of July or Labor Day rolled around, the Schwartzes and their neighbors would pool their resources to host huge block parties. At each neighborhood bash, volleyball was the neighbors' sport of choice. And, of course, Allan had no desire to sit on the sidelines. He jumped in, talked a little trash and started playing. It wasn't his favorite sport, but no matter. Allan could bump, set and spike with the best of them. When it came down to it, any game that included a ball—no matter what its size or shape—was right up Allan's alley.

Or in a pinch, a puck would suffice. When Allan was around seven years old, he took up roller hockey, and it didn't take him very long to become one of the best players on his team. His athleticism and competitive spirit more than made up for his lack of experience. Not surprisingly, he made the all-star team several years in a row. To Allan, there was nothing quite like the feeling of lining up a slap shot and, in one fluid motion, sending the puck screaming past the goalie into the net.

SCHOOLTIME BLUES

Allan attended his neighborhood school, El Rancho Elementary School, for seven years (kindergarten through 6th grade). It wasn't a bad school. But, with the exception of recess and PE, Allan hated it. To an always-on-the-move kid like Allan, the classroom was like a torture chamber. His teachers expected him to sit still in his chair and listen to boring lessons that had nothing to do with soccer, baseball or hockey. As a result, Allan's dislike for school was almost as intense as his love for sports. When it came to academics, Allan felt like a fish out of water.

Several weeks into his first-grade year, Allan's parents received some disappointing news from his teacher. Allan was having difficulty paying attention and following directions in class. When sitting at his desk, he acted like he had ants in his pants. He just *couldn't* sit still! So, Allan was scheduled for some tests with the school psychologist, and, to no one's surprise, he was diagnosed with attention-deficit/hyperactivity disorder.

According to the National Institute of Mental Health (NIMH), a child with ADHD is unable to sit still, constantly fidgets, can't concentrate on tasks, can't wait his or her turn and is impulsive—speaking and acting without thinking. That describes first-grade Allan to a tee. A full roll of duct tape couldn't have held him in his desk chair. And because Allan's impulse control was so lacking, he was also diagnosed with obsessive compulsive disorder (OCD).

Allan's parents knew something had to be done to help Allan, but they didn't want to rush into medicating their son. So, they gave Allan's school therapist permission to teach him some relaxation and concentration techniques to help him remain calm and focused in the classroom.

Unfortunately, it didn't work. Allan's fidgeting decreased slightly, and his concentration improved a bit. But the changes were negligible. So, placing Allan on medication seemed like the best "Plan B." Over the next few years, Allan's doctors prescribed several different medications. On one hand, they *did* help him with his fidgeting and concentration. But these improvements came at a cost. They brought a lot of side effects, including significant weight loss and uncontrollable motor tics in his legs, arms and face.

As the months went by, Allan's parents had to regularly weigh the pros and cons of Allan's meds. His hyperactivity had improved, but in Kim's words, "He lost so much weight that he became a shell of himself. He no longer was the Allan we knew and loved. He didn't have a passion for his sports or anything else. This was very scary and sad. So, we stopped the medication and got our son back."

On the heels of that decision, Joe and Kim made a commitment to get more personally involved in Allan's education. Kim began volunteering in Allan's classroom. She worked closely with Allan's teacher and school counselor to better understand Allan's behavior and assisted him in the areas where he most needed help. And help she did! Allan's academic performance and behavior showed steady improvement.

But much to his mom and dad's chagrin, Allan's improvement in the classroom didn't transfer to the playground. God only knows how many times Allan left his lunchbox, backpack or jacket somewhere on the school grounds. To this day Allan's parents still tease him about how many jackets he "donated" to his school. After running around and playing with his friends at lunch or recess, he just couldn't remember to pick up and bring home whatever it was that he had taken outside.

In the evenings, doing homework with Allan required the patience of a saint. His lack of interest in the "three R's" and difficulties with concentration made homework time very challenging. So, both of Allan's parents had to roll up their sleeves to share the load. Kim helped Allan with his homework until fourth grade, at which time she passed the baton to Joe. As the years went by, Joe didn't have the heart to pass the baton back to Kim. So, he remained the primary homework helper until Allan donned his cap and gown with his diploma in hand.

Along the way, Joe and Kim discovered that Allan had a real knack for one subject: basic arithmetic. He was a whiz at adding and subtracting numbers in his head. And when it came to memorizing sports stats for his three favorite Los Angeles teams—the Dodgers, Lakers and Kings—it was remarkable how many numbers he could memorize. As long as his math teachers didn't pollute math equations with abstract x's and y's, Allan excelled. So much so that his parents nicknamed him "Rain Man."

GIFTS FROM GOD?

Truth be told, Allan's love for sports and disdain for school were both gifts from God. Had it not been for his dislike of school and passion for sports, Allan wouldn't have learned to persevere at such a young age. Without the dangling carrot of sports, he wouldn't have had the drive to push through excruciating hours of classroom lectures and homework. During Allan's most unbearable mornings at school, he always had hope that something glorious awaited him at lunch time—a pick-up game of basketball, soccer or handball. And during Allan's most tedious afternoons of academic purgatory, he knew that his next playoff game was on the horizon.

Sure, Allan hated school. But his love for sports was his polar star, guiding his way through nauseating classes like social studies, life science and algebra. No matter how hard his school days were, he always had something to look forward to. Allan always had a reason to dig deep, fix his eyes on the prize and persevere.

It was true back then, and it's *still* true today.

CHAPTER 2

FAMILY, FRIENDS AND FAITH

"Love the LORD your God will all your heart and with all your soul and with all your strength. These commandments that I give you today are to be upon your hearts. Impress them on your children. Talk about them when you sit at home and when you walk along the road, when you lie down and when you get up."
-John 17:3

FAMILY

Although Allan was only five years old at the time, he remembers it like it was yesterday ... the day his little sister Shavaun was born. In the months leading up to Shavaun's birth, Joe and Kim did their best to prepare Allan for her arrival. But when he laid his eyes on her for the first time in the hospital, he had the funniest look on his face—shock, confusion and infatuation all rolled into one.

She looked so different than he had imagined ... nothing like his blonde-haired, blue-eyed mom. Shavaun's hair was dark—almost black. Her face was very petite. And her eyes: There was something unexpected about her eyes. They were deep brown and appeared slanted. To Allan she didn't look like a Schwartz. She looked almost ... Asian. But mom and dad assured him that she was theirs. So, finally convinced, Allan gave her a kiss on the forehead and welcomed into his family the most beautiful baby girl he had ever seen.

Growing up, Allan enjoyed a rare blessing that he wouldn't fully appreciate until later in life: a close-knit family that spent lots of quality time together. Not many of us can say that when we were kids, we ate three meals a day with our families. Allan can. Because Allan's dad worked from home and Kim was a stay-at-home mom, when school wasn't in session, Allan spent most mealtimes around the kitchen table with his parents, Joey, Shavaun and Kim's mom (aka, "Nana"). At times, Allan would shovel in the food in three minutes flat so that he could get back to playing outside with his friends. But—brief as it was at times—his family made their meals together a priority.

And boy did they like to eat! It didn't take long for the Schwartz family to pinpoint some of the best restaurants in Southern California. When they had a craving for Italian, Vince's Spaghetti House in nearby Ontario was their restaurant of choice. When they felt like thick crust pizza, it was worth the 35-minute drive into L.A. County to eat at Pompeii in Valinda. And one of Allan's favorite burger places was just a few miles from their house: Chino Burger. Allan loved that place—almost as much as he loved the chili cheese combo at Wienerschnitzel.

To a hyperactive young carnivore like Allan, the chili cheese combo made him feel like he'd died and gone to heaven. He could almost hear a choir of angels singing in the background as he looked down at his battle-scarred orange tray and beheld a chili cheeseburger, a chili cheese hot dog and chili cheese fries. All for him! Allan believed in God at a very young age, and, most likely, Wienerschnitzel was one of the reasons why.

When Allan was six or seven years old, he and his family stopped at a new restaurant on the way home from one of their many camping trips. Because they had never eaten there before, the eatery hadn't made it onto Allan's approved "short list." So, he wanted nothing to do with it. He was tired. He was grumpy. And he didn't like what was on the menu. So, he voiced his protest ... LOUDLY. He made it clear to anyone within earshot that he didn't want to be there. Joe and Kim gave him several warnings: "If you don't start behaving, you're going to get a spanking." Well, surprise, surprise! Allan didn't zip it.

So, Joe took him by the arm and marched him outside the restaurant. And as they made their way to the parking lot, Allan turned on the water works. He started crying and pleading for mercy—as if he was being led to the guillotine: "Please don't spank me! Please don't spank me! I'll be good! I promise!" As Joe reared back his hand to give his grumpy boy his first swat on the bottom, Allan pleaded, "No, Dad! No!" And without skipping a beat suddenly stopped crying and blurted out, "Ooh! Homemade chili cheese fries!"

Baffled, Joe thought, *Did I just hear what I think I heard? That sure came out of left field!* But then he looked up and saw what Allan had just seen a few seconds earlier: a large neon sign on the roof of the restaurant advertising one of their most popular menu items: chili cheese fries. At that point all Joe could do was laugh. They walked back inside the restaurant, and guess what Allan had to eat?

When it came to sports, they weren't just an "Allan thing." Joe and Kim made sports a "family thing." Regardless of which sport Allan was playing, his parents rarely missed a game. Neither did Allan's grandpa (Joe's dad) who all the grandkids affectionately called "Papa." In fact, Allan's Papa was such a loyal fan and supporter of Allan's teams that one year the coach presented him with a "Most Faithful Fan" trophy at the end of the season.

When Allan was in junior high, his dad took a stab at coaching. Joe volunteered as the assistant coach of Allan's baseball team for two years. He must have been good at it, because Allan's team won the championship both years. With Joe's good coaching and Allan's versatility in playing three different positions (pitcher, second base and third base), they helped lead their team to victory.

It was a time of father-son bonding that made a big impression on Allan's life.

Some of Allan's best moments with his dad revolved around sports. Since Allan was a diehard fan of L.A. sports teams, Joe purchased game tickets whenever he could fit them into the family budget. Allan and his dad attended several L.A. Kings hockey games at the Great Western Forum. And at the start of a few seasons, Joe was able to purchase a "mini plan" of Dodgers tickets that allowed him and Allan to enjoy twenty-seven games at Dodger Stadium.

For Allan, there was nothing quite like eating a "Dodger Dog" with his dad during the seventh-inning stretch with their archrivals, the San Francisco Giants, down by five runs.

Allan dreamed of one day becoming the Dodgers' starting pitcher or third baseman. That was Allan's "Plan A" when asked what he wanted to do when he grew up. But early on, Allan voiced his "Plan B." If he didn't make it onto the field as a player, he wanted to be perched in the announcers' booth calling the Dodgers' home games. Allan could see it in his mind's eye: becoming the Dodgers' next Vin Scully.

FRIENDS

When Allan and his dad weren't losing their voices at Dodger Stadium, they joined forces with the rest of their family to host some legendary parties at home. It was nothing short of remarkable how many family and friends the Schwartzes could squeeze into their 1,600-square-foot house. On one Christmas Eve, thirty family members and friends were packed into their small family room around the Christmas tree. And when it was time to open their presents, the kids tore into their gifts all at once. It was an absolute free-for-all as torn wrapping paper flew in every direction. The scene was chaotic and far too loud for most families. But not for the Schwartzes! They loved every minute of it.

And the chaos only intensified on the 4th of July. Every

summer the Schwartz family and their neighbors would block off their street to take their Independence Day parties to the next level. The neighbors would pour onto the asphalt and set up tables and chairs. The dads would drag out their charcoal barbeques and propane grills. Burgers. Hot dogs. Grilled chicken. Potato salad. Chips. Sodas. Cookies. You name it, and it was probably there on one of the many food tables. And after dark, as the patriotic music was blaring, the block exploded with sparklers and fireworks. Year after year the Schwartz family found themselves thinking, *We are so blessed to have such good friends and neighbors.*

In the days following their annual 4th of July block party, Allan took comfort in knowing he had two more months of summer vacation remaining. So, he didn't waste any of it. If he wasn't inside the house watching Boy Meets World, Teenage Mutant Ninja Turtles or his all-time favorite TV show—The Fresh Prince of Bel Air—with Joey, Shavaun and his friends, Allan and his buddies could often be found chasing down the ice cream truck. And you would think that on a hot summer's day Allan and his friends would be most interested in buying ice cream. But oh no! They knew what the ice cream man kept on the shelf underneath his freezer: stink bombs and fart bombs. Those were much more enticing than Push Ups or Choco Tacos

And with these new additions to their armory, Allan and his buddies would do something they had developed into a fine art: ding-dong-ditching. Most pranksters would be satisfied with ringing a neighbor's doorbell and running away. But not the Schwartz gang. They discovered that their stink bombs could take ding-dong-ditching to a whole new level. Their unsuspecting neighbors would answer their front doors, expecting to take in a big breath of fresh, morning air. And BAM! The stench would hit them like a ton of bricks as the nearby bushes rang with the sounds of little boys giggling. Allan loved these wince-inducing escapades so much that he often brought his little sister along. It was beneath Shavaun's dignity, but at least she got to spend some quality time with her big brother.

FAITH

Both Joe and Kim grew up in Catholic households. But as a young married couple they rarely attended Catholic Mass, and they didn't practice their Catholic faith at home. Nonetheless, when Joey, Allan and Shavaun were babies, Joe and Kim did the "Catholic thing." They attended mass on special occasions like Christmas Eve and Easter Sunday, and they had their kids christened by a Catholic priest.

But in the months following Shavaun's christening, God began to stir in Kim's heart. She became tired of having a stale faith that involved nothing more than going through the motions and jumping through certain religious hoops. She longed to have a personal relationship with her Creator and Savior, Jesus Christ. So, in 1994, when Allan was just six years old, Kim prayed a prayer to accept Jesus Christ as her Savior and Lord. She asked Christ to forgive her sins, come into her life and lead her life from that point forward. She was so excited that she told Joe all about it. And it didn't take long for him to make the same decision.

Both Joe and Kim drew a line in the sand and made the decision to place Jesus Christ in the driver's seat of their lives *and* their family. And they knew that if Jesus was going to be their new top priority, church needed to be prioritized as well. So, the Schwartzes started attending Calvary Chapel Chino Hills on Sundays, which served as their home church for almost ten years. Although today the church tops 10,000 in weekly attendance, it was much smaller when the Schwartzes called it home in the 1990s. But it was exciting for them to watch their church grow right before their eyes

Unfortunately, not everyone in their family shared their excitement. Since six-year-old Allan had ants in his pants, sitting through a church service on Sunday mornings was not his idea of a fun weekend. But thankfully, Joe and Kim stuck to their guns. Not being above bribes, Joe and Kim discovered a great way to motivate Allan to stop fussing about going to church: Food!

Allan knew there was a pot of gold at the end of every sermon ... even the most boring ones.

Most Sundays after church, Joe and Kim would take the kids to West Coast Bagels for lunch. Not only were their bagels hot, fresh and tasty; West Coast also made the best bagel sandwiches. Allan loved sitting around a table with his family sinking his teeth into a scrumptious bagel sandwich. It was honestly his favorite part of Sunday mornings.

That being said, Pastor Jack Hibbs *did* make an impression on Allan at a young age. Sure, his sermons were rather long and pulled Allan away from the Sunday football programming on ESPN. But by the time Allan was eleven or twelve, he came to like the fact that Pastor Jack had firm convictions about the Bible, and he wasn't afraid to stand up for what he believed. Week after week, Pastor Jack spoke of God's love, mercy and forgiveness. And he urged everyone to have a personal relationship with Jesus Christ. Allan didn't understand it all, but gospel seeds were being planted in his mind and heart that would be watered and grow in God's perfect timing.

After Allan completed his middle school years at Magnolia Junior High School, Joe and Kim made the decision to send him to a private Christian school. It was important to them that he be surrounded by strong Christian role models who weren't restricted from talking about God and the Bible in class. And Allan's parents wanted to provide him with more opportunities to make Christian friends who would help him steer clear of the destructive pitfalls that fun-loving teenagers like Allan tend to fall into.

As with any important decision, it required a certain amount of sacrifice. But Joe and Kim counted the cost and enrolled Allan in Western Christian School in the nearby city of Upland. At first, Allan was disappointed that he wouldn't be attending high school with his neighborhood friends. And he wasn't thrilled about the forty-minute-one-way ride to school on the city bus. But Allan decided to be a good sport and give it a go. And it's a good thing he did, because it didn't take long for both Allan and his parents to realize that Allan was right where he needed to be. God's hand was in it. Those gospel seeds had been lying dormant inside Allan long enough, and God was getting ready to send down the rain.

During the fall semester of Allan's sophomore year, a certain high school freshman caught his eye. Priscilla was smart and funny, and Allan thought she was *so* cute. They quickly became friends, and as Halloween approached, Allan got up the nerve to ask her out. She was flattered, but said she had a prior commitment—helping with her church's Halloween youth party. She invited Allan to come, so he enthusiastically said, "Sure!" Allan felt Cupid's arrow sail right through his heart. For the first time in his life, he couldn't *wait* to go to church.

On Halloween night Allan's parents gave him a ride to Priscilla's church, Calvary Chapel Chino Valley. Allan's head swirled with thoughts of what the night would be like with his new heartthrob. But the night didn't go *anything* like Allan had imagined. Priscilla spent most of her time with her other friends. However, that turned out to be a blessing in disguise. Allan's time was freed up to make a few new guy friends and get to know the church's great youth pastor, Pastor Dustin.

After a follow-up "Let's just be friends" conversation, the writing on the wall became clear. Allan's romance with Pricilla was over before it had ever really started. But for Allan, her simple invitation to church had been life-changing. Allan began attending Pastor Dustin's youth group at least twice a week. And when Dustin spoke about Jesus Christ and salvation, Allan soaked it up like a sponge. For the first time in his life, Allan started to *love* times of worship. Although he couldn't carry a tune in a bucket, Allan memorized the words to the praise songs, and he sang them as loudly as if he and God were the only two people in the room.

Allan had always *believed* in God. He had always had a certain amount of *respect* for God. But now, Allan really *cared* about God. He *loved* God, and He never wanted to leave God's presence. It was at this point that Allan chose to follow Jesus Christ as his Savior and Lord. He humbled himself and invited Jesus to travel the eighteen inches from his head to his heart. Allan opened his heart and invited Jesus in. And he has never been the same since that day.

God's Spirit began moving in Allan's heart in a clear and powerful way. Allan's quick temper and new-found habit of swearing didn't disappear overnight. But there was no doubt that God was doing something special inside Allan. Allan's prayers weren't stale or routine. They were fresh and heartfelt. At times the tears would flow down Allan's cheeks as He prayed. His worship was passionate and unhindered. And he no longer paid attention to the sermons and Bible studies because he was *supposed* to. He paid attention because he *wanted* to. He was inspired. He was motivated. He was hungry for God. In a culture where many young Christians "faked it to make it," Allan Schwartz was the real deal.

His *faith* in God's Word was real. His *hope* in God's goodness was real. His *love* for God's Son was real. And they *had* to be real! Because as the greatest trials of Allan's life were fast approaching, only a *real* faith, a *real* hope and a *real* love for God would give Allan the strength and fortitude he would need to persevere.

CHAPTER 3

HIGH HOPES AND DESERT DREAMS

"See, I am doing a new thing! Now it springs up; do you not perceive it? I am making a way in the desert and streams in the wasteland."
- Isaiah 43:19

SWEET 16

As Allan approached the end of his sophomore year, he had more friends than any teenager should be allowed to have —friends from the neighborhood, friends from school, friends from his sports teams and friends from church. And three of his best friends from his church youth group, Tiffany, Matt and Dan, had a great idea. They wanted to throw Allan a surprise sixteenth birthday party ... the biggest one ever. They just had two small problems: They had no money, and they didn't have a house big enough for such a record-breaking celebration.

Well, neither did Joe and Kim. But ... no matter! When Allan's parents heard his friends' sales pitch, they were all in. So, in the days leading up to the big party, Joe cleaned the pool, Kim rented an inflatable boxing ring, and the adolescent party-planning committee spread the word discreetly to all of Allan's friends. On the day of the party, Allan walked through his front door and received the shock of his life when over forty of his friends yelled, "Surprise!"

Some of the boys had already gotten permission from Joe and Kim to carry out the first crazy prank on the birthday boy. They proceeded to grab Allan, drag him into the backyard and throw him into the swimming pool. And, of course, Allan's friends couldn't let *him* have all the fun, so they jumped in right after him. So began the best birthday party of Allan's life. He loved every minute of it: the swimming, the food, the boxing, the food, the presents, the food, the laughter and—you guessed it—the food.

Later in the evening, Allan and his friends crammed into the garage, where one of his buddies pulled out his guitar and started playing worship songs. And Allan and his forty friends spent an hour singing praises to God. As Kim heard their singing and peeked into the garage to witness their spontaneous chorus of worship, she became misty-eyed. She thought to herself, *I am so blessed to have these young teenagers in my home choosing to praise and worship the Lord, not because they have to, but because they want to.* It was a day neither Allan nor his parents will ever forget.

THE BIG MOVE

To many Christians, the success of Allan's birthday party would seem to be a sign from God that the Schwartz family was exactly where He wanted them to be. Well, maybe they were. But that didn't necessarily mean that He wanted them to stay there. Just as God Himself moves in mysterious ways, He often moves His followers in mysterious ways. Such was the case with Allan and his family.

In Kim's words, "God was orchestrating a solution even before we realized there was a problem." In the months leading up to Allan's sixteenth birthday, Joe and Kim started to get a gnawing feeling that their days in Chino were coming to an end. At first it seemed unthinkable. After all, they *loved* their home, their neighbors and their church. And all three of their kids had grown up in their little slice of paradise on Amber Road. But the feeling wouldn't go away. After several months, they became convinced that God was leading them to sell their home and move. But where?

Around this time, Joe and Kim were on a short vacation—just the two of them. As they traveled north on Interstate 15 above the Cajon Pass, they passed through the city of Victorville. Unexpectedly, traffic came to a standstill, and California Highway Patrol officers began escorting all northbound vehicles off the freeway. (It turns out a semitruck had overturned on the freeway, blocking all three lanes.) As Joe and Kim followed the detour, they stumbled upon the town of Apple Valley. Although Apple Valley had gained some notoriety in past years as the long-time home of Hollywood's "King of the Cowboys"—1950s movie star Roy Rogers and his wife, Dale Evans—Joe and Kim had never heard of it.

But they really liked what they saw. Apple Valley was small and semi-rural, and the homes were a fraction of the price of those in Chino. So, Joe and Kim called a family meeting and announced, "Kids, we're moving to Apple Valley!" The idea sounded a little crazy to Allan, but he figured that if God was behind it, it would work out. So, Joe and Kim put their Chino home up for sale, and it sold in just three days. And they were able to turn around and purchase, dollar-for-dollar, a home in Apple Valley that was much larger than their Chino home and came with an acre of land.

As icing on the cake, the local Christian high school, Apple Valley Christian School (AVCS), was just three miles from the Schwartzes' new home. So, for Allan, the days of boarding the city bus for a forty-minute-one-way ride to school were a thing of the past. A quick, five-minute drive, and Allan was walking through the front gate of Apple Valley Christian School.

Now, going from a school of five hundred students to a school with only nineteen kids in his class took some getting used to. But as always, Allan made friends quickly and had a blast shooting hoops with the boys at lunchtime. Little did he know that his days of swishing three pointers, scoring goals and rounding third base were quickly drawing to a close. In fact, in a matter of months, his family's greatest nightmare would begin.

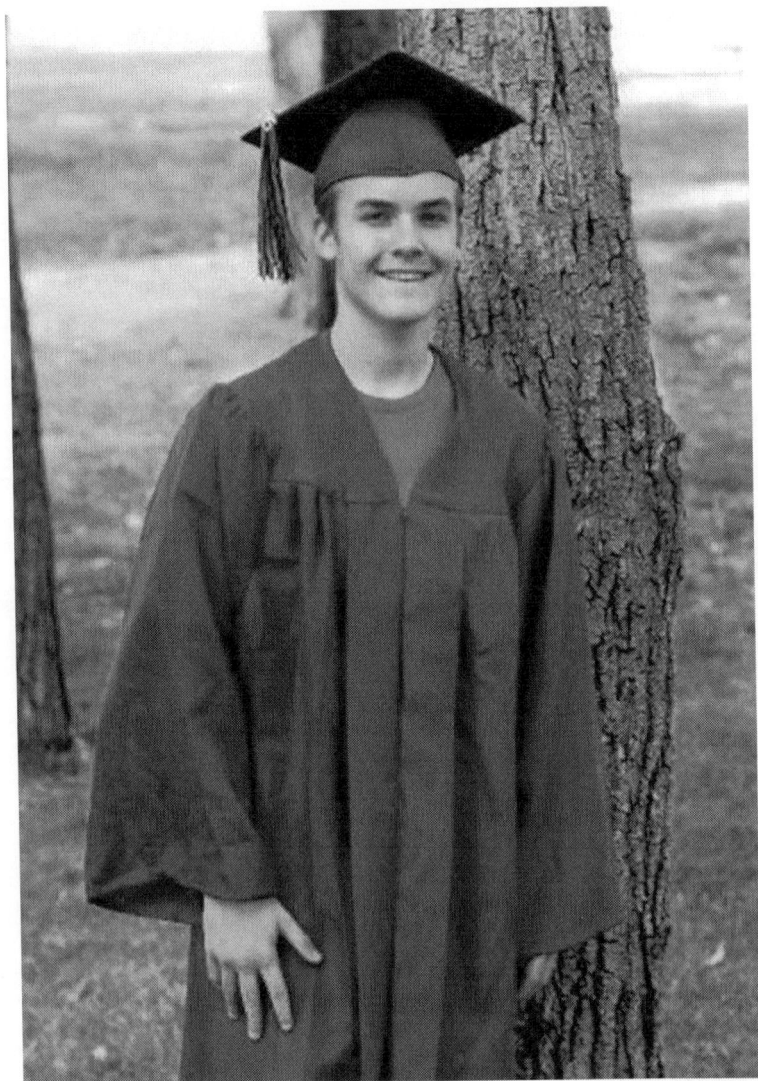

Just weeks after his first major back surgery, Allan graduates
from high school.

PART TWO

ARACHNOID WHAT?

CHAPTER 4

HERE COMES THE PAIN

"I am in pain and distress; may Your
salvation, O God, protect me."
- Psalm 69:29

In the rearview mirror, Allan's sweet sixteen party seemed like a lifetime ago. It was hard to believe that it had been just over a year since he and his friends had been making human-powered whirlpools in his backyard pool and taking swings at each other in the inflatable boxing ring. What he had been doing effortlessly just a year earlier seemed impossible by the end of 2005.

Early in his senior year, Allan was at school doing what he normally did at lunchtime: playing basketball with his friends. But this time something unexpected happened. Allan and one of his friends collided and fell to the ground ... Allan first, and then the other kid. And just one thing broke the other kid's fall: Allan's left wrist. In prior years, tumbles like this had been no big deal. Allan would just stand up, brush himself off and get back to the business-at-hand on the court.

But this time was different, and Allan knew it almost immediately. Pain shot through his wrist every time he moved it in a certain direction. A few hours later, the x-ray at the emergency room revealed what Allan and his parents already suspected. His wrist was broken, and his basketball-playing days were over ... at least for six weeks.

To Allan, wearing a cast for a month and a half felt like wearing a strait jacket for a year. But eventually his six weeks of being sidelined came to an end, and Allan was back on the basketball court. However, almost as soon as he made his grand return, he noticed his back was hurting. At first, he chalked it up to a pulled muscle. *That's what I get for sitting on my butt for the past six weeks! But it'll go away in no time.* Allan's pain *had* to go away. After all, there was no backup plan. He was Allan Schwartz. Varsity sports star ... future Los Angeles Dodger ... Mr. Invincible.

Initially, Allan kept the pain to himself and prayed it would go away. But as days passed into weeks, it *didn't* go away. Quite the opposite. Instead of getting better, it got worse ... much worse. So, Allan had no choice but to break the news to his parents. Allan's pain became so severe that he couldn't walk without the most intense level of pain (a 10 out of 10 on the pain scale) shooting through his lower back and legs. And within a few weeks, Allan was confined to a wheelchair. In just a month's time, his life had been turned upside down, but neither Allan nor his parents were going to go down without a fight. Sure, he was missing lots of school, but a team of wild horses wasn't going to stop him from graduating in the spring. One way or another, Allan was bound and determined to get out of that wheelchair and back on his feet.

In the early weeks of 2006, Joe and Kim took their seventeen-year-old son to several different doctors—specialists in their fields who evaluated him and scheduled him for a series of MRIs. The doctors determined that Allan had a large, herniated disc that was pinching all the nerve roots between his L5-S1 vertebrae. There was no doubt in their minds that these pinched nerves were the source of Allan's back and leg pain.

It seemed clear to the neurosurgeon that Allan needed surgery, but as is often the case, the Schwartzes' health insurance company disagreed. They required a less expensive option to be tried first: at least two epidural injections of anesthesia administered into Allan's lower spine. In some cases, epidural injections bring significant relief from the inflammation and pain of a nerve-pinching, bulging disk.

So, Allan didn't put up a big fuss. Although he was skeptical, like a good patient he jumped through the medical insurance hoops placed in front of him and underwent not two but *three* epidural injections. But he soon regretted it. Not only did the epidural injections *not* help, they actually made Allan's pain worse. You see, the injections are given during a fluoroscopy, a medical procedure that takes place in two steps. First, a solution containing an opaque dye is injected into the back. Next, x-rays are passed through the body at specific time intervals to provide real-time videos that track the flow of the fluid. This allows the doctor to pinpoint the best site for the epidural injection.

In most patients, a fluoroscopy is a harmless procedure. After a few hours, the dye-filled solution dissipates in the body without any complications. But Allan wasn't so lucky. Years later, Allan and his parents would learn that in a very small number of patients, some of the earlier dyes used in fluoroscopies can remain in the cerebrospinal fluid for years, even decades, after the procedure. Research has shown that some of these earlier dyes may contribute to incurable diseases like arachnoiditis.

Sadly, neither the three epidurals, nor acupuncture, nor physical therapy made a dent in Allan's pain. Meanwhile, an MRI showed that his herniated disk had grown so large that he was at risk for permanent paralysis if surgery wasn't performed immediately. Allan was terrified by the notion that he might never walk again. Never be able to walk with his senior class to receive his high school diploma. Never be able to run onto a basketball court or soccer field. Never be able to stroll to the front of the church on his wedding day. Never even be able to walk to the bathroom.

So, when a world-renowned neurosurgeon at Cedars-Sinai Medical Center in Los Angeles said, "Allan, we don't have a moment to lose," Allan and his parents quickly agreed to proceed with the surgery. With just a few short months remaining before graduation, Allan underwent a laminectomy and discectomy. In plain English, his herniated disk was removed, and part of his lower vertebrae was removed with it.

During the surgery, Joe and Kim nervously paced the floor of the nearby waiting room, prayed, and hoped for the best. After what seemed like an eternity, the doctor emerged from behind the waiting room doors and gave them the report. The herniated disc was worse than he had expected—so bad that it had adhered to the nerve roots in Allan's lower back. The doctor also told them that Allan's recovery would take longer than expected. That being said, they could expect that, in time, Allan should be able to resume most of his prior activities. To Allan's two worried parents, that was music to their ears.

After he came out of recovery and heard the good news, Allan could finally take a big sigh of relief. He was on the road to recovery. But at the same time, he figured he'd better take advantage of the perks Cedars-Sinai's surgical wing had to offer—especially the personal butler and the gourmet meals prepared by world-famous chef Wolfgang Puck's staff.

The very next day, the physical therapist had Allan taking his first steps in weeks—albeit with a whole lot of pain. A few days after that, Allan was released from the hospital to go home where his brother, sister and Nana Ann were excitedly waiting for him. Almost immediately, Allan's family could tell that his pain level had improved.

Through God's grace and his physical therapists' hard work, Allan slowly resumed his old routines in the weeks that followed. He put away his wheelchair and returned to school. Just a few weeks after turning eighteen, Allan was grateful to walk across the stage with his fellow Apple Valley Christian School seniors to receive his high school diploma. He was well on his road to recovery. The pain was finally behind him. Or so he thought.

CHAPTER 5

"IT'S ALL IN YOUR HEAD"

"You are worthless physicians, all of you!
If only you would be altogether silent!
For you, that would be wisdom."
- Job 13:4-5

In Psalm 119:116, the psalmist cries out to God, "Sustain me according to Your promise, and I will live; do not let my hopes be dashed." And King Solomon writes bluntly in Proverbs 13:12: "Hope deferred makes the heart sick." Despite the rosy prognosis offered by his surgeon, primary care doctors and physical therapists, it didn't take long for Allan's hopes to be dashed and his dreams of a healthy future to be shattered. The most heart-wrenching two years of Allan's life were about to begin.

Less than a year after his spinal surgery, Allan's pain returned out of nowhere and hit him like a freight train. No red flags. No gradual onset of symptoms. No warning.

It was Valentine's Day, 2007. Like most other days, Allan was watching a rerun of The Fresh Prince of Bel-Air, and Kim asked if he could help her wash a few windows. Since it was Valentine's Day, Allan thought it was the least he could do for his sweet mom. So, he grabbed a rag with one hand and the bottle of Windex with the other and set to work to make the windows sparkle. But without any warning, Allan lost all strength in his hands and legs. The bottle of Windex slipped out of his hand as a searing, level-10 pain shot through his body from his neck to his toes. He cried out for his mom as his hands began turning as blue as the Windex he'd just been spraying.

Kim tried to warm up Allan's hands with a heating pad, but it didn't work. She gave him ibuprofen for his pain, but that didn't work either. So, she helped him into the car and rushed him to St. Mary Medical Center in Apple Valley. But after running a battery of tests, the doctors were at a loss to explain what was happening. They had never seen anything like it. Allan's symptoms were seemingly unexplainable.

And his symptoms only grew worse with time. Allan's family noticed that he was growing weaker, and he began spending more time in bed. So, Kim called the surgeon's office and scheduled a follow-up appointment for Allan. When the day of the appointment arrived, they drove back to Cedars-Sinai, where Allan was subjected to another battery of tests. After examining the results, the doctor told Allan and his parents the last thing they wanted to hear: "There's nothing more I can do." That was that. No recommendations. No alternative treatments. No referrals. And no real answer to Allan's nagging question: "What's wrong with me?"

Allan was only eighteen years old, yet he was losing hope. He honestly didn't think he would make it to his twentieth birthday. The pain was *that* bad. His situation seemed *that* hopeless. With each new day, it felt like something new was happening to his body—something even worse than the day before. Walking became so painful for Allan that he had to return to his wheelchair. His parents put extra large grips on his silverware, because he didn't have the strength to grasp a fork or spoon without them. Allan lost the ability to dress himself, shower himself or even walk to the bathroom. He soon found himself completely immobile ... confined to his bed for six straight months.

Because of damage to the nerves controlling his bladder, on

half a dozen occasions, Allan lost the ability to control his bodily functions. As a result, he had to be given a urinary catheter. While necessary, the catheters only increased Allan's physical agony.

To help manage the pain, Allan was prescribed Lyrica (a strong nerve pain medication), Prednisone (a steroid that reduces inflammation) and OxyContin (one of the strongest prescription pain killers available). But none of these drugs made a significant dent in Allan's pain. He was seen by at least fifty different doctors at St. Mary Medical Center, Cedars-Sinai Medical Center, USC Medical Center, UCLA Medical Center, UCI Medical Center, Loma Linda University Medical Center and several other Southern California hospitals.

The doctors subjected him to multiple x-rays, MRIs, PET scans, spinal cord stimulators and muscle biopsies. Allan had to go to the lab and do blood work more times than he could count. And to make matters worse, his small veins made it almost impossible for the technicians at the lab to draw blood on the first try. After two or three needle pokes per visit, Allan began to feel like a human pin cushion.

He underwent several nerve conduction studies (NCSs) to determine whether his nerves were working properly. Although most patients experience very little discomfort during the study as electrical impulses are transmitted through their bodies, the procedure was very painful for Allan.

A few of Allan's doctors experimented with Intravenous Immunoglobulin Infusions (IVIGs)—a three-hour procedure that involves a slow IV drip of antibodies harvested from healthy blood donors' plasma. The procedure was uncomfortable and even painful, but Allan was a no-pain-no-gain kind of guy. So, once again he pushed through the pain.

After several treatments, Allan stood up and took a few slow steps. It felt like a breakthrough. Unfortunately, it didn't last. Within a day or two Allan could no longer walk, and further IVIG treatments didn't restore what he had lost. The IVIGs didn't increase Allan's mobility or reduce his agony.

At one point, doctors at Loma Linda University Medical Center gave him weekly epidurals, hoping they would curb his back pain. Unfortunately, they had the opposite effect. On one occasion a medical student administered Allan's epidural, and he made a rookie move: He hit a nerve. Allan's pain shot through the roof, soaring to a whole new level. His back was never the same.

At one point during the medical rat race, Joe and Kim decided to get Allan out of the house and take him to the food court at the local mall. As they wheeled Allan in, he knew what he wanted: some good stir fry steak from Mongolian Grill—so much better than a burger from McDonald's. But a few bites into his meal, Allan started choking. His throat was so swollen from inflammation that he had a hard time swallowing. For Allan, even the simplest of pleasures was no longer simple *or* enjoyable.

Allan felt so defeated. He constantly cried out, *Why, God? Why are You putting me through all this pain? If I've done something to deserve this, tell me what it was. I don't understand this pain, and I can't take it anymore!* One day as Allan was at one of his lowest points, the tears started streaming down his cheeks. He asked Kim, "Why me, Mom? Was it because I was so hyper and such a hard kid to raise? Was it something I did?"

These questions broke Kim's already-fractured heart. As tears welled up in her own eyes, she said something Allan would never forget: "Allan, you are a *great* kid! You don't deserve this pain, and I'd take it from you if I could."

God has created each of us with a remarkable ability to endure suffering, *if* we know and understand the reason for it. But what made Allan's ordeal so unbearable was the absence of real answers. His back was killing him, and some of the best doctors in Southern California didn't know why. At the age of twenty, he had less mobility than many ninety-year-olds. Yet no amount of medical tests could explain the source of the problem. Allan's true diagnosis was a mystery.

Some medical professionals took a stab at a diagnosis. One doctor told Allan that he had Raynaud's Disease, a condition where spasms in the blood vessels of the hand restrict blood flow to the fingers. Of course, that doctor's diagnosis was wrong. So too was the diagnosis offered by a nurse at UCLA Medical Center, who pulled Joe and Kim aside and said, "I know what this is. I've seen it before. It's bone cancer." Scared half to death, Kim immediately summoned the doctor who told them in no uncertain terms, "I don't know what he has, but I know it's *not* bone cancer."

The misdiagnoses were frustrating and at times terrifying. But worst of all was hearing this message from several of Allan's doctors: "It's all in your head." Because Allan's bloodwork, MRIs, CAT scans and PET scans didn't reveal a known disease, and because none of Allan's medications seemed to dull his pain, doctors who were unable to think outside the box came to the conclusion that there was only one logical explanation: Allan's pain wasn't real. It was imagined.

Unbelievable! All the trips to the lab, doctor visits and hospital stays seemed to be doing more harm than good. Allan was taking handfuls of medications every day that weren't curbing his pain. His parents were now several hundred thousand dollars in debt from his medical bills. And what did Allan have to show for it? A hopeless, idiotic statement ringing in his ears like a broken record:

"It's all in your head."

CHAPTER 6

BRUCE: A FRIEND IN LOW PLACES

*"Two are better than one, because they have
a good return for their work: If one falls down,
his friend can help him up. But pity the man
who falls and has no one to help him up."*
– Ecclesiastes 4:9-10

Every hospital has its good days and bad days, its good reviews and its bad reviews. UCLA Medical Center is no exception. Over the years, the doctors and nurses at UCLA have saved the lives of thousands of their patients who would be quick to sing their praises. Unfortunately, Allan's two-week stay at UCLA in the spring of 2008 was rough, to say the least.

No doubt, the nurses were less than thrilled when Kim told them she would remain with Allan 24/7 during his hospital stay. But Allan's "Mama Bear" wouldn't have it any other way. And it's a good thing! She was on hand the night Allan had an adverse reaction to a Fentanyl patch. His heart began racing a mile a minute. Allan felt like his heart was beating out of his chest, and it was only after threatening to take matters into her own hands and pull the patch off herself that the nighttime nurse caved in to Kim's demands. Crisis averted. That one incident made sleeping on a stiff-as-a-board hospital chair for two weeks well worth Kim's effort.

So much of what took place during Allan's hospital stay seemed pointless. The spinal taps ... pointless. The bloodwork and MRIs ... pointless. The nurse-turned-doctor who misdiagnosed Allan as having bone cancer ... pointless. And the doctors who tried to make the case that Allan's pain wasn't physical but psychological—all in his head—utterly pointless. Allan had been given *no* new answers, *no* effective new treatments, and he was in *no* less pain. It felt like an utter waste of two weeks.

But thankfully, when it comes to working in His followers' lives, God doesn't waste anything. And that was certainly true at UCLA. It turns out that God's purpose for Allan being at UCLA was much different than Allan had assumed. Allan thought he was going to UCLA to meet a team of doctors who could change his life. But instead, God placed him in a hospital room with a Christian roommate who changed his life.

Bruce was admitted to UCLA Medical Center with Stage 4 Renal Carcicoma (kidney cancer). His prognosis was grim, but he was determined *not* to give up without a fight. At best, the chemotherapy and radiation were just buying him a little time before the inevitable happened. Bruce was terminal. He was dying, and he knew it.

But Bruce didn't *look* like a dying man. And he certainly didn't *talk* like a dying man. Like Allan, he was energetic, talkative and had an amazingly cheery perspective on his pain and suffering. His positive outlook was infectious, so he and Allan became instant friends. Over the next week and a half, Bruce and Allan spent many hours talking, laughing and sharing their struggles with God. Allan was an open book with Bruce. He held nothing back. He admitted that He didn't understand what God was doing. And he confessed that, at times, he was angry at Him. His pain just didn't make sense.

Bruce patiently listened and shared how he himself had wrestled with God. Like Allan, he had many questions, and, on more than one occasion, he had given his Creator a piece of his mind. But in recent months, God's Holy Spirit had given him a peace— a peace that can't be fully understood or explained. Bruce was convinced that God is loving, strong and always at work for the good of those who love Him and are called to do His work (Romans 8:28).

Bruce assured Allan that God could heal him in a second if He chose to. But if He didn't, He must have a different plan—a *better* plan for him. And Bruce was convinced that as a follower of Jesus Christ, it was his job to walk in faith—to trust God 100%, believing that He was somehow, someway working out His master plan. Bruce had decided to trust and obey God no matter what—even at times when God's plan didn't seem to make sense.

In the midst of his nightmarish hospital stay, there were moments when Allan felt as if there was an angel of God lying in the bed next to him. Bruce's words pierced his heart and touched the deepest part of his spirit in a way that few people's words ever had. Allan knew that God had hand-picked Bruce to be his room-mate so that he could speak God's strength, hope and persever-ance into his life. And in that hospital room, Bruce carried out his God-given assignment so well. He spoke life into Allan, and he watered the seeds of faith and perseverance inside Allan that have influenced so many believers in years since.

On the day Bruce was released from the hospital, Allan started to tear up—feeling he was losing his best friend. He knew he would have to brave the remaining days of his hospital stay on his own. But now he was better equipped to do so ... because of Bruce.

In the months that followed Bruce's release from UCLA, Allan kept in contact with him by phone. Whenever Allan and Bruce chatted, they picked up right where their prior conversation had left off. Bruce continued to speak strength, hope and perse-verance into Allan's life. His spirit was strong. But as the weeks went by, his voice became weaker and weaker, until he reached a point where he couldn't talk on the phone anymore. Knowing how much Bruce meant to Allan, Bruce's wife, Barbara, and his daughter, Sam, kept Allan in the loop, giving him regular updates on Bruce's condition.

One day Barbara called Allan to thank him for the most recent family photos he had mailed to Bruce. She told Allan how grateful she was that he had taken the time to send them to her. But something seemed off. Allan could tell from the sound of her voice that she was struggling to hold back the tears. And it turns out ... she was. Just one day before Allan's photos had arrived in the mail, Bruce breathed his final breath here on earth and entered eternity.

From a *human* perspective, Bruce lost his battle with cancer. But both Allan and Barbara clung to their *eternal* perspective: Cancer might have won the battle, but Bruce had won the war. He had fought the good fight. He had finished the race. And through it all he had kept his unwavering faith in God. And now he was in the presence of His Savior and Lord Jesus Christ, where he would hear Him speak the six awe-inspiring words that all followers of Christ long to hear: "Well done, good and faithful servant."

CHAPTER 7

THE DIAGNOSIS

"Those who sow in tears will reap with songs of joy.
He who goes out weeping, carrying seed to sow, will
return with songs of joy, carrying sheaves with him."
- Psalm 126:5-6

In 2007 and 2008, Allan was bedridden—continuing to take handfuls of pain medication every day that weren't working. And in the aftermath of the California housing market crash of 2007, Joe's income as a mortgage lending agent had plummeted. So, the Schwartzes' financial situation had gone from bad to worse. They were on the verge of losing their home, and Joe and Kim's marriage was struggling. There were no more block parties, no more camping trips, no more father-son outings at Dodger Stadium. Even simple trips to Wienerschnitzel were a thing of the past. Life as the Schwartzes had known it was over. And hope was quickly fading.

Every day that Allan and his parents woke up, they were forced to relive the nightmare. Allan's health didn't improve from day to day. Just the opposite—it deteriorated. He could no longer use his walker to get around the house. So, he became dependent on his dad and mom to help him get to bathroom, take a shower and eat. Allan was caught in a downward spiral of pain and immobility, and neither he nor his parents could do anything about it. It felt as if a thick cloud of hopelessness was hovering over their family, and they prayed to God that it would go away. Yes, they wanted Allan to be healed. But more than anything else, they just wanted answers—insight into what was causing Allan's pain and how to fix it. But no answers came.

As hopeless as Allan's situation seemed, his parents refused to give up hope. So, they began drafting emails and sending short home videos to Los Angeles-based news stations, hoping they would feature Allan in an upcoming "mystery diagnosis" segment. Perhaps one of these television stations could help connect Allan with a doctor who would be willing to think outside the box and put in the hard work necessary to correctly diagnose Allan's disease.

Normally, when Kim's mom, Nana Ann, started to cry about Allan's health crisis, Kim would console her and tell her to hold back the tears. But when it came time to film the home video that would be sent to the networks, Kim told her mom to cry her eyes out if it would help Allan get the help he desperately needed. And wouldn't you know it—God used Nana Ann's tears in a powerful way.

Shortly after Allan's 20th birthday, Joe was contacted by ABC News. The station wanted to run a health segment on Allan, hoping that a doctor or medical facility would view it and offer Allan a much-needed path to a diagnosis and cure. Although the initial broadcast didn't result in incoming phone calls from doctors, the broadcast recording provided Kim with a powerful tool to send to doctors and medical centers.

Since Allan had already been seen by specialists at some of the best medical facilities in Southern California, Joe and Kim sent Allan's medical records and the ABC news story to specialists in world-renowned medical facilities around the country. They had high hopes that Allan's case would be accepted by the medical experts at The Mayo Clinic in Rochester, Minnesota. After all, the Mayo Clinic medical team specializes in diagnosing and treating rare diseases. But because Allan had already been seen by experts at three highly-regarded hospitals, they were unwilling to accept Allan as a new patient.

Undaunted, Joe reached out to Johns Hopkins Hospital in Baltimore, Maryland. And it's a good thing he did. His persistence joined forces with Nana Ann's tears to move the heart of God *and* the hearts of the doctors at Johns Hopkins. Joe and Kim received a return phone call from Dr. McArthur, the director of Johns Hopkins' neurology department. The Schwartzes were thrilled to learn that he had personally viewed Allan's segment on ABC News, and he was willing to admit Allan for comprehensive testing with the goal of providing a diagnosis and treatment plan.

Dr. McArthur made arrangements to have Allan, Joe and Kim flown out to the hospital for five days. Best of all, he arranged to have Allan's co-pay and co-insurance waived. It was such a relief to Joe and Kim to know they wouldn't be getting any pesky calls from medical bill collectors in the months after Allan's visit to Johns Hopkins. But Dr. McArthur's kindness went even further. He gave Joe and Kim meal vouchers for five days. And after hearing that Joe and Kim only had $400 to their name, he allowed them both to stay in Allan's room for the duration of Allan's time in the hospital. This single act of kindness saved their family several thousand dollars in motel costs.

You see, five days turned into five and a half weeks. Just like the teams of doctors at Loma Linda, UCLA and USC, Dr. McArthur and his team found themselves struggling to find the root cause of Allan's unusual symptoms. Every day for two weeks, doctors examined Allan, performed scans and researched their medical journals to offer something that Allan and his family had long prayed for and sought: an accurate diagnosis. And after two weeks at Johns Hopkins, that's exactly what Dr. McArthur and his team gave them.

Allan and his parents will never forget the day Dr. McArthur and his team filed into Allan's hospital room and rather abruptly said, "We have a diagnosis." You could have heard a pin drop. After two years of experiencing hell on earth, dealing with a level of pain that Allan wouldn't wish upon his worst enemy. After being subjected to more MRIs, PET scans, spinal taps and epidurals than he could count. And after being told over and over, "It's all in your head," Allan and his family would finally be able to call his silent torturer by name.

Dr. McArthur glanced at Allan and spoke these life-altering words: "You have arachnoiditis." Arachnoid what? Neither Allan nor his parents had ever heard of this disease. They knew what an arachnid is: a spider. But what on earth is arachnoiditis? And why was it causing Allan so much pain?

Dr. McArthur went on to explain, "Arachnoiditis is a rare, incurable disease that causes inflammation of the arachnoid layer of the membrane that surrounds the spinal cord and brain. The job of the arachnoid layer is to transport fluid around the brain and spinal cord. But when it gets inflamed, it causes severe pain." He went on to say that epidurals and back surgeries can contribute to the onset of the disease. And, like it or not, at twenty years old Allan was the youngest patient that Johns Hopkins had ever diagnosed with the disease. In fact, at that point in time, Allan was the youngest person in the United States with arachnoiditis.

As Allan and his parents' heads were swimming—trying desperately to wrap their minds around what they were being told —Dr. McArthur answered the question that was on everyone's mind: *Is there a cure?* Without hesitation he said, "There is no cure, only treatments for the symptoms. And if the disease spreads to Allan's brain, it could be fatal." At that point Kim couldn't hold back the tears any longer. She started to break down as she made a beeline for the door. Joe followed quickly behind, and together in the hospital hallway they held each other and began crying out in prayer, *Lord, what are we supposed to do now? How can we fix the unfixable? What do you want us to do?*

They were relieved that, at long last, Allan's disease had been given a name. But at the same time, they felt overwhelmed by a sense of helplessness. Joe pulled out his cell phone to relay the doctor's diagnosis to Joey and Shavaun, who were nervously waiting for an update back home. And by the time Joey picked up the phone, an unexplainable peace began to settle over Joe and Kim. Joey and Shavaun listened patiently, asked a few questions, and then Joey spoke the words that Allan's two worried parents desperately needed to hear. "Mom, Dad, God said that Allan is going to be okay."

Joe and Kim finished their phone call with a few final words and "I love you's." Meanwhile, unbeknownst to them, Allan was in his hospital room having an encounter with God. He was praying, but it wasn't a typical prayer where *we* do all the talking and *God* does all the listening. Allan was speaking to God, but God was also speaking to Allan. Among other things, God reminded Allan of His words in Joshua 1:9—inspiring words that would soon become Allan's favorite verse in the Bible: "Have I not commanded you? Be strong and courageous. Do not be terrified; do not be discouraged, for the LORD your God will be with you wherever you go."

Back in the hallway, Joe and Kim wiped away their tears as they stepped back into Allan's room. To their surprise, they found him lying in bed smiling ... almost beaming, as if his prized Dodgers had just won the World Series. They walked over to Allan's bed and said, "Allan, we have something to tell you..." But before they could voice another word, Allan blurted out, "Mom and Dad, I know what you're going to say. But God already let me know that I'm going to be okay ... no matter *what* the doctors say."

To Allan and his parents, it felt like they were on holy ground. Allan's agonizing journey had not been in vain after all. His pain had a source, and that source had a name: arachnoiditis. And more importantly, his pain had a purpose. Neither Allan nor his family knew what that purpose was. But God had made it abundantly clear that Allan would be all right, because—just like in

Bruce's life—God was at work for the good. And at that point in time, that's all they needed to know.

The first thing Allan wanted to do was to open his laptop and begin playing worship music. So, Joe handed him his laptop, and within a few seconds, Chris Tomlin's song, "God of This City," was blaring in his room. The lyrics expressed so well what Allan and his parents were thinking and feeling at that moment:

You're the light in this darkness
You're the hope to the hopeless
You're the peace to the restless
You are

There is no one like our God
For greater things have yet to come
And greater things are still to be done in this city!

As Allan worshiped his Lord in one of the best ways he knew how—by singing along with Chris Tomlin—the tears rolled down his cheeks. And this time they weren't *sad* tears. They were tears of relief and tears of unexplainable joy. As strange as it sounds, lying in that hospital bed 2,500 miles from home, Allan felt as if he finally knew God's plan for his life. God wanted him to become a motivational speaker—sharing his testimony of God's goodness and grace in the midst of his pain. God had inspired Allan to be strong and courageous, trusting and worshiping His great and awesome God in the eye of the storm. And God was calling Allan to inspire others around him to do the same.

CHAPTER 8

LET'S GET TO WORK

"Jesus said, 'Go home to your family and tell them how much the Lord has done for you, and how He has had mercy on you.'"
- Mark 5:19

Now that Allan and his doctors knew what they were dealing with, it was time to get to work reclaiming the independence that Allan had lost. Dr. McArthur wasted no time moving Allan to a different floor of the hospital that specialized in recovery and treatment. He was assigned to a team of highly-skilled physical and occupational therapists who worked with him several hours every day, strengthening muscles that had atrophied while Allan was bedridden and teaching him how to fend for himself at home. Their goal was clear: Help Allan re-learn most of the basic skills necessary for him to live a safe, independent life.

Over the next three weeks, the physical and occupational therapists at Johns Hopkins taught Allan how to more safely transfer from a bed to a chair and back again. They showed him techniques for getting dressed independently, how to shower and how to answer the call of nature without assistance. Like a sponge, Allan soaked in all he was being taught. And like Rocky Balboa facing the pummeling Russian giant, he trudged through the pain, pushing his body to its limits.

The first time he showered himself, he screamed in agony. Using certain muscles that he hadn't used in months caused them to shriek in protest. But Allan's unyielding, what-doesn't-kill-you-makes-you-stronger attitude paid off. As the days at Johns Hopkins passed, he showed remarkable improvement.

Unfortunately, Allan's encouraging progress came at a cost. His initial five-day hospital stay turned into more than five weeks. That was a long time for Allan, Joe and Kim to be crammed into a small hospital room. And that was, by far, the longest stretch of time they had ever spent away from Allan's older brother and his younger sister, who was only fifteen years old. This was especially hard on Kim, who missed Joey and Shavaun terribly. She knew she was where she needed to be, but she longed for her family to be together again.

As the family's breadwinner, Joe worried and prayed ... prayed and worried. After all, flying to Maryland for a five-day hospital stay with only $400 in their family's checking account required a leap of faith. But trying to stretch that same $400 over a period of five weeks required more than just faith. That required a five-loaves-and-two-fish kind of miracle.

And that's exactly what God gave them—but not before He taught them to pray harder and trust Him more. After the first five days in Baltimore, Joe and Kim ran out of meal vouchers. So, they began discussing ways to ration their $400 to sustain them as long as possible. But even their four measly "Ben Franklins" disappeared in the first week.

Someone had fraudulently used the Schwartzes' debit card and overdrawn their account. Although the bank promised to replenish their stolen money, they said it could take up to thirty days. To survive in the meantime, Joe and Kim needed a miracle more than ever. They didn't want to burden any of their family or friends with their financial woes. So, they just prayed hard and trusted God to provide.

And He *did* provide. Over the next four weeks, God's provision came through in remarkable ways. One day a nurse came into Allan's room with a few bags in her hand. After some light chitchat she said, "I'm not sure why, but when I went grocery shopping today, God asked me to buy you these things." Tears came to Kim's eyes as she reached for the bags of groceries—tasty sustenance that had arrived in the nick of time.

A few days later, another nurse brought Joe and Kim the best doggy bag they'd ever received: several servings of her should-be-world-famous, homemade fried chicken. Even cold, it tasted amazing. As Joe and Kim sank their teeth into that little taste of heaven, it was yet another reminder that God was with them. On other days, other nurses brought in desserts: pie, cookies and pastries. No doubt, there were a few days when there was nothing to eat, but those days were few and far between. Joe and Kim were on track to lose a few pounds during their hospital stay, but they definitely *weren't* going to starve.

The Christian nurses at Johns Hopkins brought Allan and his parents more than just food. They also brought them small gifts of kindness that sparked hope. Nurses like Lynn, who had a talent for painting. When she learned that Allan's favorite Bible verse was Joshua 1:9, she painted the verse onto a small canvas and presented it to Allan during her next shift. Allan and his parents were so touched by her gift that they kept it beside Allan's bed for the remainder of his hospital stay.

LIVING OUT HIS CALLING

It was one thing for Allan to *believe* God had called him to share his testimony of God's grace and goodness, but it was quite another to *live out* that calling. So God didn't waste any time giving Allan an opportunity to speak grace, hope and perseverance into hurting people's lives—hurting people like Ed.

Allan met grumpy old Ed in physical therapy. He was suffering from a malignant brain tumor. He was mad at the world, frustrated with his doctors, and he made it clear that he wanted *nothing* to do with God. During the first few days that Allan and Ed were in physical therapy together, they didn't speak a word to each other. But as it turned out, Ed was watching Allan and noticed his unusually positive attitude, even when grimacing from severe pain. He *longed* for what Allan had.

Curiosity eventually got the best of Ed. Finally he asked, "Allan, what's your secret?" Without skipping a beat, Allan responded, "My secret is Jesus Christ."

Ed wouldn't have tolerated that answer coming from anyone else. But he took it to heart when it came from Allan. Almost immediately, Allan and Ed became friends. They looked forward to seeing each other at physical therapy and bumping into each other in the hospital hallway. For the first time in a long time, Ed smiled and even laughed a little. And his new buddy—a twenty-year-old bundle of hope and positivity—was getting him to reconsider what *really* mattered in life.

One day, out of the blue, Ed sent word to Allan that he wanted him to stop by his hospital room. So, as soon as it was convenient, Joe and Kim wheeled Allan down the hallway and into Ed's room.

In typical Ed fashion, he didn't mince words. He abruptly asked Joe and Kim to leave and close the door so he could talk privately with Allan.

Joe and Kim didn't know whether to be insulted or terrified. Why was he so insistent that they leave the room? Should they be concerned for Allan's safety? They had a dozen questions, but they didn't want to make a scene. So, they reluctantly filed out of Ed's room and waited nearby, just in case.

Allan was almost as confused as his parents. But he hoped for the best and rolled with it. After some initial conversational pleasantries, Ed took a deep breath and spat out what he had wanted to say. "Allan, before I saw you in physical therapy, I had no hope. But after seeing you fight, you gave me hope." And what Ed said next almost took Allan's breath away: "I want to become a Christian and follow Jesus."

Allan could hardly believe his ears. Of all people ... Ed. Crotchety, mad-at-the-world, disgusted-with-God Ed wanted to trust in Jesus Christ as his Savior and Lord!

Allan was beside himself, and he told Ed so. Allan asked him a few questions, explained what he was about to do and then led him in a short sinner's prayer: proclaiming his belief in Jesus Christ, asking Jesus to forgive his sins and declaring his desire to follow Him as Lord for the rest of his life.

After reaching the "Amen" of their prayer together, Allan opened his eyes and beheld a new man—a better man. No, Ed wasn't crying like a baby or breaking into a chorus of "Amazing Grace." But he had a peace about him that he hadn't had before. His face seemed brighter, his burden lighter.

Almost as quickly as the conversation began, it ended. Joe and Kim returned and wheeled Allan back to his own room. As they did, Allan shared with them the miracle that had just happened, and together they joined the chorus of angels in heaven celebrating Ed's new life in Christ. A sense of peace flooded Allan's heart as he thought: *Even if Ed loses his battle with cancer, he will make it to heaven, because he gave his life to Jesus Christ. God chose me to lead my new friend to Jesus, and now he is a changed man.*

Ed's change came none too soon. Within a matter of days, Ed was gone. He lost his physical battle with cancer. But in the midst of the battle, he had gained something infinitely more valuable: forgiveness, peace with God and eternal life. He was the first of thousands of men, women and children God would place in Allan's path to encounter the amazing grace and goodness of God.

WE'RE COMING HOME!

As Allan's grueling five and a half weeks at Johns Hopkins wrapped up, he had a new lease on life. For the first time in six months, he was able to walk short distances with a walker. He could safely get himself to and from the bathroom. With the help of special utensils, he could feed himself, dress himself and take showers without assistance. And for the first time ever, Allan was leaving a hospital with prescription medications that didn't take a buckshot approach to pain management. Medications that targeted the source of his pain were maintained; others that had too many side effects were discontinued. There was still plenty of hard work left to do, but Allan was ready to go home.

He was physically ready. But more importantly, he was emotionally and spiritually ready. Like Joshua after receiving his marching orders from God, Allan felt strong and courageous. His mystery disease had been pulled out of the shadows and exposed by the light. Best of all, Allan knew and understood God's purpose for his life more clearly than ever before. His pain *finally* had a purpose. And for the first time in three years, Jeremiah 29:11 finally made sense: "'For I know the plans I have for you,' declares the LORD, 'plans to prosper you and not to harm you, plans to give you hope and a future.'"

As Allan and his parents pulled into their driveway after their lengthy pilgrimage to Johns Hopkins, they enjoyed the sweetest family reunion in the history of Schwartzdom. Allan and his parents savored every moment wrapping themselves in the hugs of Joey, Shavaun and Nana Ann. The smiles, the food and the "Welcome Home!" signs were all wonderful. But best of all was the moment when the whole family saw the miracle with their own eyes. Allan stood to his feet and was noticeably stronger, more energetic and radiating with renewed hope for the days ahead.

CHAPTER 9

A HAIL MARY PASS

"I lift up my eyes to the hills—where does my help come from? My help comes from the LORD, the Maker of heaven and earth."
- Psalm 121:1-2

Life was good ... difficult, but good. Allan couldn't put into words how amazing it was to be able to do, once again, what most of us take for granted: getting dressed, brushing his teeth, feeding himself, and scooting to and from the bathroom. By this point in his journey, Allan didn't have any fanciful ideas of playing point guard for the Lakers or becoming the Dodgers' next starting third baseman. He was just grateful for what God *had* given him: basic mobility and relief from the worst of his pain.

Once Allan and his parents were home, all three of them breathed a collective sigh of relief. But there was no time to let their hair down or take a much-needed vacation. They knew they had to hit the ground running. There was work to do. Allan had to acclimate to his new regimen of medications and continue his physical therapy exercises. Kim had to get their home back in order after her long absence. And Joe had to keep his nose to the grindstone—working like a madman to get the family's finances back on track.

And their hard work paid off. As the weeks went by, a bit of normalcy began to return to their family. But as had been the case time and again over the past three years, their normalcy was short-lived. About a month after his return from Johns Hopkins, Allan noticed that his progress had plateaued. He made no claims to being an expert on arachnoiditis, but it seemed odd to him that his mobility wasn't improving. And the medications—although they were supposed to target his pain with greater precision—weren't curbing his pain any better than they had in the hospital.

Sadly, things went from bad to worse. At the three-month mark, Allan's pain pendulum began swinging in the wrong direction. Over the past few years, Allan had developed a high tolerance for pain. On the ten-point pain scale, Allan could handle the "fives" and "sixes" without letting out so much as a whimper. He could even take the occasional "sevens" and "eights" in stride. But his mobility began to decrease as his "level-ten" pain came back with a vengeance. It became increasingly difficult for Allan to get out of bed, use his walker or get dressed, because the pain that radiated from his neck down to his toes was excruciating.

So, in early 2009, after several failed attempts to get any satisfying answers from Johns Hopkins, Kim did what she did so well: With dogged determination, she surfed the internet for answers. Every day she spent several hours making phone calls, sending emails and researching treatments for arachnoiditis. But since it was such a rare disease, she found herself hitting dead end after dead end. So, when it seemed as if Kim had tapped all the medical expertise in the United States, she started looking overseas for answers—even when those answers were unorthodox. Even in places that the FDA wouldn't touch with a ten-foot pole.

In her research she discovered a German neurosurgeon who, according to many medical professionals, was the world's leading expert on arachnoiditis. At the Paracelsus Klinik in Zwickau, Germany, Dr. Warnke had perfected a surgical procedure for patients suffering from Allan's disease, a procedure called thecaloscopy. This spinal surgery involves placing a very small scope (video camera) and tiny surgical tools between two of the three layers of the spinal column, allowing the surgeon to perform a very intricate but minimally-invasive surgery. The procedure had risks, but it was showing promising results for many men and women suffering from arachnoiditis, reducing their pain and increasing their mobility. It wasn't a cure, but it was the closest thing to it.

Kim figured Allan had nothing to lose, so she reached out to Dr. Warnke and sent him Allan's ABC News story. Allan and his family began praying that he would respond. And within a few days, Kim was thrilled to see his email response in her inbox. Dr. Warnke asked for Allan's medical records, so Kim and Joe sent them immediately.

Allan hoped for a response within a day or two, but a few days turned into several weeks. Because of the time difference, scheduling difficulties and the language barrier with Dr. Warnke's staff, it took some time to have a follow-up phone conversation. But it was worth the wait. Over the phone, Joe and Kim shared their financial hardships with Dr. Warnke. They held nothing back, even though they feared their transparency might scare him off. But to their delight it had the opposite effect. He agreed to perform the thecaloscopy on Allan—free of charge. That was a *huge* answer to prayer that would save the Schwartzes thousands of dollars. But Dr. Warnke was quick to point out he didn't have the authority to waive the hospital charges or the cost of airfare to and from Germany.

Still, the Schwartzes accepted Dr. Warnke's generous offer and started praying harder than ever for God to make the unaffordable become affordable. And, once again, God came through in a big way. Allan and his parents sent the details of Allan's story to Lufthansa Airlines in hopes they would cover the cost of the flight. They were delighted to receive word back that the airline would fly Allan, Kim and one other family member to and from Germany free of charge. It was a roundtrip miracle!

And the miracles kept pouring in when Joe's dad, Papa Allan, sent Kim a high-limit credit card and asked her to use it for *all* their expenses in Germany. Once again God had come through in an incredible way. Allan and his parents now had a way for all the expenses—the airfare, the hospital stay, the surgery, and all incidental expenses—to be covered.

Just to be safe, Kim reached out to Dr. McArthur at Johns Hopkins for a second opinion about Allan undergoing the thecaloscopy. Dr. McArthur wasn't familiar with the procedure since, at the time, it wasn't being used in the United States. But after researching the procedure and the groundbreaking work of Dr. Warnke, he came to the conclusion that the benefits of the surgery would likely outweigh the risks. So, he expressed his support of Allan's decision to travel 5,800 miles to Zwickau to give it a try.

So did Allan's family. Unfortunately, Joe wouldn't be able to join them for the trip. Finances were too tight, and they couldn't afford for their income to come to a crashing halt again, the way it had during their five-and-a-half weeks in Baltimore. Even with the cost of the surgery and airfare covered, the trip would be expensive, and the bills back home would keep pouring in. So, the most supportive thing Joe could do was to stay home and keep working. In his absence, Kim's sister Debbie stepped in to join Allan and Kim for the long trip to Germany.

Some might say it was a longshot. Others might call it a Hail Mary pass. But if Allan believed there was hope a quarter of the way around the world, he was willing to do what it took to take hold of it. Allan believed with all his heart that with God all things are possible, especially when Christ's followers believe—really BELIEVE—and are willing to take a leap of faith (Matthew 19:26). So, shortly after his twenty-first birthday, Allan was ready to take his biggest leap of faith ever ... a leap of almost 6,000 miles to a little-known town beyond where the Berlin Wall once stood. It seemed like a strange place for a miracle. But Allan had grown accustomed to anticipating God's miracles in the most unlikely places.

CHAPTER 10

GERMANY OR BUST!

*"Even youths grow tired and weary, and young men stumble
and fall; but those who hope in the LORD will renew their
strength. They will soar on wings like eagles; they will
run and not grow weary, they will walk and not be faint."*
- Isaiah 40:30-31

THE UNFORGETTABLE TRIP

"It was brutal!" Even years later, that's how Allan describes the twelve-hour flight from Southern California to Germany. The three free tickets from Lufthansa Airlines were a blessing, but Allan's pain level was almost unbearable. Every bit of turbulence sent shockwaves up and down his spine. No matter how much he fidgeted and repositioned himself, he just *couldn't* get comfortable. It was, without a doubt, the hardest flight of his life.

When the plane finally touched down in Germany, Allan blurted out, "Thank God!" Unfortunately, the international airport was several hundred miles from Zwickau. So, the final stretch of Allan's day-long trip involved a short connecting flight on a twenty-seat commuter plane and a two-hour train ride into Zwickau. Allan had never ridden on a plane that was *that* small, or on a train with employees who were *that* bad-tempered.

Once the train left the station, one of the female employees approached Allan, Kim and Debbie and asked them a few questions in German. Baffled, Kim and Debbie tried to explain that they didn't speak German. But the attendant became more and more agitated as they didn't answer her plain-as-the-nose-on-her-face questions. Several of the passengers sitting nearby started chuckling as they overheard the comedy of errors. It turned out that several of them spoke English, but they refused to step in and translate. Eventually one of the commuters turned to Kim and said, "She needs to see your credit card." Crisis averted.

With each stop the train made, passengers filed out. And as Allan looked out the window, it appeared they were going deeper and deeper into the desert. He turned to his mom and asked, "Are we going in the right direction? This hospital must be in the middle of nowhere!" With no other passengers remaining, the train made its final stop. And before Kim and Debbie could even ask if they were in Zwickau, a man grabbed the handles of Allan's wheelchair and whisked him down the loading ramp and up the railway platform.

Allan's porter was a German version of Speedy Gonzales—pushing Allan so fast that Kim and Debbie lost sight of him as he made a hairpin turn in front of the locomotive. Kim and Debbie grabbed their luggage and ran as fast as their loaded-down legs could carry them, trying desperately to catch up with Allan and Speedy. Thankfully, once they rounded the front of the train, they could see Allan and, as an added bonus, civilization! The sight of buildings was a welcome relief.

No one would have claimed that Allan's two-week trip to Germany was off to a dull start. Once Kim and Debbie caught their breath, they realized their hotel wasn't within walking distance of the train station, so they hailed a taxi. It was no Rolls Royce, but after the first three legs of their trip, it was the closest the three of them got to four-star transportation. Unlike the hotel they were about to check into, at least the taxi had air conditioning.

Living in the High Desert town of Apple Valley, Allan and his family had become accustomed to desert heat. But the heat in Germany was different—not dry like back home but muggy, sweat-streaming-down-your-back humid. Although Kim and Debbie weren't thrilled to learn their hotel room didn't have air conditioning, they shrugged it off and decided to make the most of the few hours of daylight remaining. After all, it was Sunday, and Allan wasn't scheduled to meet with Dr. Warnke until the following morning.

Since the hotel was a short walk to the hospital, the three of them took the opportunity to get the lay of the land. They had worked too hard to get to where there were to chance getting lost on their way to the hospital. So, they set out from the hotel and made their way through the centuries-old village of Zwickau, parts of which dated back to the thirteenth century. As they made their way to Paracelsus Klinik, they soaked in the sights around them. The architecture of some of the older buildings was gorgeous, spawning comments like, "Wow! They don't make them like *that* anymore!" And "We're not in Apple Valley anymore!"

To everyone's surprise, the streets were paved with cobblestone. For most tourists, it would be a dream come true, walking down the centuries-old cobblestone streets of a quaint village in the former East Germany. But Kim and Debbie quickly noticed something: Pushing a grown man in a wheelchair across cobblestone streets is really, really hard. And for a man with arachnoiditis, bouncing up and down cobblestone roads in his wheelchair was worse than medieval torture. With every turn of his wheels, Allan grimaced in pain.

A German man passing by noticed that Kim and Debbie were struggling to push Allan's wheelchair in a straight line. (They were zigzagging down the street like they'd been nipping the schnapps.) He approached the three of them and asked if he could help. Or ... at least that's what Kim and Debbie thought he was asking. After all, they couldn't understand a word he said. So, Kim reached into her purse and pulled out a picture of the hospital. He recognized it and proceeded to help push Allan the rest of the way to the clinic. And while he was pushing, he was able to show off the five English words that he knew: "Big, fat, white, American pigs!"

Lesson learned! Evidently, some East Germans aren't big fans of Americans. So, for the remainder of their two-week trip, Kim and Debbie claimed to be Canadian. And it worked like a charm.

THE UNFORGETTABLE SURGERY

Although Allan, his mom and Aunt Debbie were exhausted from their grueling 5,800-mile trip to Zwickau, sleep was hard to come by that night. Too many thoughts were racing through their heads about the day to come. Would the language barrier with the hospital staff create difficulties? Would Dr. Warnke go through with Allan's surgery, and if so, would it work? Would this finally be the life-changing miracle they had prayed for, or would it be yet another disappointment?

The following morning, Kim and Debbie pushed Allan down the cobblestone streets once again to the Klinik, where Allan was admitted. And thankfully, many of their worries and concerns were alleviated as soon as they met Dr. Warnke. A peace came over them, knowing they were in the right place at the right time. Dr. Warnke was down-to-earth, friendly and much more understanding and compassionate than most of Allan's prior doctors had been. And, without a doubt, he had a much better handle on Allan's disease and the difficulties it presented to both him and his family. He asked Allan what kind of career he wanted to have, and a curious smile came to his face when Allan replied, "I want to be a motivational speaker." Perhaps he didn't understand the word "motivational."

Dr. Warnke sat with Allan, Kim and Debbie for more than

thirty minutes, explaining Allan's treatment plan step by step. His first priority was to relieve the majority of Allan's pain. To Allan and his mom, that sounded too good to be true. So, Kim chimed in, explaining that there was no way to relieve Allan's pain with medication. For several years various doctors had prescribed every pain pill imaginable to Allan, and the results were always the same. They either didn't work, or they made him tired and loopy. Dr. Warnke politely listened but then responded, "Oh, you don't know what drugs we have here. I *will* get him out of pain."

After pulling out Allan's bag full of prescription drugs and showing them to Dr. Warnke, the look on his face spoke volumes. He couldn't *believe* any doctor with half a brain had prescribed so many different pills. At that moment Dr. Warnke said what his second priority would be: to get Allan weaned off every medication he had been taking. In Dr. Warnke's opinion, they were doing him more harm than good, making his arachnoiditis pain even worse.

A few minutes later, a nurse wheeled Allan to his room, which would be his home base for the next two weeks. Just a few minutes after he was settled in his bed, a nurse put an IV in his arm and began administering medication. Allan couldn't believe the difference. He wasn't sure what it was that his doctor had told the nurse to slip into his IV bag, but he didn't really care. Within just a few minutes of receiving his IV, his pain level dropped dramatically. And he didn't nod off or feel like a space cadet. That by itself was a miracle.

In the three days that followed, Dr. Warnke ran many tests, making sure he had a clear picture of Allan's vertebrae and spinal cord before performing the thecaloscopy. He also wanted the first few days of detox to run their course, allowing Allan's body to acclimate to a new normal without so many pills.

Several times each day, Dr. Warnke came into Allan's room to check on him. During one of these check-up visits, he asked Kim and Debbie where they were staying. After naming the hotel, he offered them a much better alternative—one that included, among other things, air conditioning. Dr. Warnke was aware of the Schwartzes' financial difficulties, and Allan's hospital room was large. So, he instructed his staff to bring two more beds into the room so that all three of them could be together for the remainder of Allan's hospital stay.

They couldn't have asked for a better arrangement. Night and day, Allan had his biggest support system just a few feet away. And the new arrangements saved the Schwartzes a bundle on travel expenses, especially after Dr. Warnke sweetened the deal by covering the cost of *all* their meals in the hospital. Never mind the fact that the hospital food was terrible. At least it was free!

At the three-day mark, Allan was ready for his surgery—at least as ready as he'd ever be. But a last-minute MRI revealed that Allan's herniated disc, which had been surgically repaired three years earlier, had adhered to the nerve roots of his lower spinal cord. No wonder Allan's pain was so intense! So, Dr. Warnke broke the news to Allan that he would have to perform two surgeries. In addition to performing the thecaloscopy, he would also have to repair Allan's bulging disk. Since the news was broken to Allan just minutes before his surgery, he didn't have enough time to stress over it. His world-renowned doctor was confident that it was the right thing to do, so that was good enough for Allan. After all, God hadn't led him this far to let him down now.

The dual surgery took about three hours. When Allan was in recovery, Dr. Warnke gave Kim the good news that she had prayed for. The surgery had gone smoothly, and they could expect to see improvement in Allan's pain level and mobility within a matter of hours. Once again, it seemed too good to be true. But Kim and Debbie held onto the hope that they weren't being sold a bill of goods from an overconfident doctor. They longed to see Allan back to his old self again. Time would tell.

Three days after surgery, the nurses were able to help Allan get out of bed. At first, his pain was intense. But with each passing day, his pain level *decreased* as his mobility *increased*. With several rounds of physical therapy every day, Allan made steady progress.

By the end of his first week in Germany, Allan already felt like he had a new back, and as a result, a new lease on life. He felt stronger than he had felt in a *long* time.

And as Allan made his way through his second week at Paracelsus Klinik, it seemed clear that his surgery had been a miracle. By God's grace, Dr. Warnke had accomplished both of his goals. Allan was completely weaned off his old medications. And more importantly, Allan's pain was lessening with each passing day—allowing him to be more physically active than he had been in several years.

He was standing erect and walking without assistance. He shuffled slower than a ninety-year-old man on Jupiter, but, praise God, he was walking! Kim called home every day and excitedly shared Allan's progress with Joe, Joey and Shavaun. As his second week in Germany came to a close, Allan was able to do many of the things that he hadn't been able to do in ... he couldn't remember how long: sleep through the night, climb out of bed, walk to and from the bathroom and even walk up and down stairs. Allan and his family were praising God that after three long years, his miracle had finally arrived.

As Allan and his mom said their final goodbyes to Dr. Warnke before being discharged from the hospital, they thanked him to the point of embarrassment. When the doctor was able to get a word in edgewise, he gave Allan a few final instructions and words of encouragement. He urged him to continue doing physical therapy several times each week. And he assured him that, in time, he would be able to do anything and everything he wanted to do without limitations.

GOODBYE ZWICKAU

Allan's return trip from Germany was a walk in the park compared to his brutal trip getting there. For starters, Luftansa Airlines upgraded Allan's seat to business class, which allowed him to fully recline. That by itself made the twelve-hour flight more comfortable and relaxing. But the biggest difference was Allan's post-surgery back. His overall pain level had plummeted, and his range of motion was better than it had been at any point since high school. He could sit, stand, lift his arms and even walk without experiencing ANY level-10 pain. The surgery was working, and—as an added bonus—his new, downsized cocktail of prescription drugs was working.

As Allan's plane touched down at LAX, he and his mom could hardly wait to walk off the plane and let Joe and the rest of the family see his miracle with their own eyes. His return from Johns Hopkins had been sweet, but his return from Germany was even sweeter.

As the car pulled into the driveway, Joe, Joey, Shavaun and Nana Ann were all standing there waiting for him. They could hardly believe their eyes as Allan opened his car door, stepped onto the driveway and walked several steps to where they were standing. Nana Ann was first in line for a hug, and she almost crushed Allan with her embrace.

The hope and joy that flooded that driveway somehow surpassed the emotion of Allan's return from Johns Hopkins less than a year earlier. More than ever before, everyone believed in their hearts that Allan had received his miracle. And they hoped to God that *this* time their hopes wouldn't be dashed.

Allan at the Hansa Center

PART THREE

THE VALLEY

CHAPTER 11

BACK ON AMERICAN SOIL

"Blessed are those who dwell in Your house; they are ever
praising You. Blessed are those whose strength
is in You, who have set their hearts on pilgrimage."
- Psalm 42:4-5

E ven though Allan and Kim had only been away from home
for a third of the time they had spent in Maryland, their
return from Germany felt better ... more like a miracle. Back when
Allan returned from Johns Hopkins, Allan's family could see that
he was much better than before. But this time, they looked at him
in stunned amazement, convinced he was healed.

In the months that followed, Allan continued his physical
therapy several times a week. And he seemed to be getting
stronger with each visit. Standing, walking, grasping, throwing
and catching—Allan was doing it all. His physical therapists
couldn't believe he was the same Allan they had seen just weeks
earlier grimacing in pain whenever he attempted to do even the
simplest of tasks. But now, at the age of twenty-one, he was able to
do so much more with so much less pain. He was even doing leg
lunges.

Allan and Kim both wondered at times if the physical therapists were pushing him too hard. But then they remembered what Dr. Warnke had said: "You can do anything and everything you want to do without limitations." So, whatever Allan felt comfortable doing, that's what he did. Within a short time, Allan began doing the things he had done before the onset of his illness: chores around the house, church with his family and concerts with his friends. He even began dating a girl named Brittney Hernandez.

Joe and Kim couldn't put into words how good it felt to see their son living life again, enjoying so many of the activities that he hadn't been able to do over the past three years. He wasn't rounding third base or sinking fast-break layups, but people who didn't know Allan weren't able to tell he had a debilitating disease that had confined him to a wheelchair earlier that year. Unless he or one of his family members told them, they didn't know he was a walking miracle.

But to everyone's disappointment, his miracle was, once again, short-lived. Coming back from Germany, Allan and his family had hoped and prayed for a long-term miracle. Not that they prayed specifically for God to give him seventy, fifty or even thirty years of good, pain-free health; but they had prayed that his surgery would give him *years*, not *months*, of good health and mobility. But *months* is all God gave him. And that would lead to one of the Schwartzes' greatest challenges of all: working through their frustration and disappointment with God.

Like most Christians, when Allan and his family read the accounts in Scripture of Jesus opening the eyes of blind Bartimaeus (Mark 10:46-52), healing the ten lepers (Luke 17:11-19) and raising Lazarus from the dead (John 11:17-44), they fixed their thoughts on the fact that these men were miraculously healed by God. But they didn't give much thought to what inevitably happened to these men years later: Their health deteriorated, and they died. Such is the case with *all* miracles of physical healing. They are temporary. And the temporary nature of God's healings can, at times, be very hard to wrap our minds around.

In early 2010, about six months after Allan's surgery, his back and leg pain returned. Mild at first, but as the days passed—just like after his first back surgery in Southern California and his treatment at Johns Hopkins—his pain intensified.

Kim reached out to Dr. Warnke and explained Allan's symptoms. He sounded concerned, and he wanted to examine Allan himself. It turned out Dr. Warnke was scheduled to attend a Southern California medical conference in the next few weeks, so he graciously agreed to see Allan while in town.

When the day came, Allan and his parents made the two-hour drive to Los Angeles where, just as he had promised, Dr. Warnke met with Allan. He gave Allan a basic examination, but he seemed disengaged, as if his mind was already back home in Germany. Dr. Warnke spoke to Allan and his parents in a matter-of-fact way. He wasn't cold or rude, but he didn't seem as concerned or as caring as he had been in Germany. To everyone's dismay, he didn't offer any *real* solutions or new treatment plans to tackle Allan's health crisis. He just kept saying, "Allan, you should be able to do anything you want to do. You just need to keep moving and doing physical therapy."

To Allan and his parents, that medical advice was about as helpful as a doctor telling him to brush his teeth and drink lots of water. Of course, he was going to keep moving! Of course, he was going to keep going to physical therapy! That was the whole point of reaching out to Dr. Warnke in the first place: Movement and physical therapy had stopped working, and if the trajectory of his pain didn't change fast, he would soon be right back where he started. Back in a wheelchair. Back in bed. Back in agony.

As Allan's appointment with Dr. Warnke came to a close, a sense of utter defeat and despair crept in like a dark cloud filling the room. No doctor on the planet understood arachnoiditis as well as Dr. Warnke, yet even *he* seemed baffled by Allan's deteriorating health. Dr. Warnke had given Allan all the *right* medication. He had performed the *right* surgery and had given him the *right* physical therapy regimen. But for some unknown reason, what had worked with his other patients wasn't working as well with Allan. So, like it or not, Dr. Warnke's bottom line was coming across loud and clear. The world's leading expert on arachnoiditis was telling Allan in no uncertain terms: "There's nothing more I can do for you."

CHAPTER 12

A TICKET TO MAMA CARPINO'S

"The angel of the LORD came back a second time and touched him and said, 'Get up and eat, for the journey is too much for you.'"
- 1 Kings 19:7

After leaving Dr. Warnke the first time, Allan had a new lease on life. So, the 4,000-mile trip from Germany wasn't so bad. But after meeting with him the second time, the two-hour drive home from Los Angeles felt like a long, drawn-out death march. Allan had an incurable spinal cord disease that caused him debilitating pain. And the world's best and brightest neurosurgeons had all reached the same conclusion: nothing was going to change that fact. No matter how hard Allan and his family fought arachnoiditis, the end result would remain the same: Arachnoiditis would win.

No matter how many specialists he saw, no matter how many treatments he was given, no matter how much physical therapy he did, no matter how many hundreds of thousands of dollars he and his family spent, it ultimately wouldn't matter. Allan would *live* in pain, and he would one day *die* in pain. It seemed clear at the time that even his most faith-filled, fervent prayers wouldn't change that fact. Could God heal Allan? Both Allan and his parents would have answered that question with an unequivocal "Yes!" But for some unexplainable reason, God chose *not* to heal him. For Allan and his family, God's purpose and plan for him didn't make sense. Especially when Allan's condition continued to go downhill.

Despite his best efforts to keep walking, within a few weeks of his follow-up appointment with Dr. Warnke, Allan was back in his wheelchair. He wasn't back on wheels because he was lazy or because he enjoyed getting the best parking spots at Target. And it certainly wasn't because Allan had a low tolerance for pain. By this point in his life, Allan could push through level-7 and level-8 pain better than most of us could handle pain at a level 4 or 5. A pain that would cause us to double over and call 911 was just an *average* day in Allan's life.

Thankfully, as the months passed and 2010 came to an end, Allan didn't regress to the point of being bedridden or having to be assisted with dressing himself, brushing his teeth, going to the bathroom or taking showers. But the intense pain prevented him from walking, which severely hindered his mobility and brought many of his recreational activities to a crashing halt. No more driving. No more hiking. No more walking up stairs. No more easy access to church, restaurants or concerts. Sure, a wheelchair could take Allan to a lot of the same places he liked to go with his family and friends. But his wheelchair was a poor substitute for his formerly-healthy and pain-free back and legs.

Allan's situation looked dire, and his discouragement ran deep. He'd come to question whether it was even worth pursuing any new attempts at treatment, only to be met with more disappointment. But he couldn't sit by in self-pity. For one thing, it wasn't in his nature—especially as he saw his mom, once again, roll up her sleeves to scour the internet looking for a needle of hope in the haystack of hopelessness. Allan and his parents were cut from the same cloth. Undaunted determination ran through their blood. And maybe God wasn't done providing miracles just yet.

To no one's surprise, Kim's diehard, no-retreat-no-surrender resolve paid off yet again. First, Kim arranged for Allan to undergo Intravenous Nutrient Therapy—sometimes called a Myers' Cocktail. A port was inserted into Allan's chest, and at predetermined intervals he was given pharmaceutical-grade vitamin and mineral supplements: high doses of vitamin C, calcium, magnesium and B vitamins. The doctors hoped the supplements would reduce the inflammation in his back that was contributing to his pain. At first, the injections seemed to do just that. Allan's pain level decreased for a few days, but it returned in short order.

Next, Kim discovered hyperbaric oxygen therapy (HBOT), which involves breathing pure oxygen in a chamber where the air is pressurized two to three times higher than normal air pressure. During this procedure, a person's lungs gather more oxygen, which is carried in the bloodstream throughout the body. HBOT has been used for decades for decompression sickness. But in recent years, researchers have discovered that when our blood carries extra oxygen throughout our bodies, it can help stimulate stem cells that promote healing.

At the time, HBOT was considered "experimental" and required special approval by Allan's insurance company. But thankfully, Allan was approved for a round of treatments. And he could do them at nearby St. Mary Hospital, which was less than a ten-minute drive from his house. Unfortunately, after more than a half dozen HBOT treatments, neither Allan's pain level nor his mobility improved. So, Kim scratched that one off her checklist and kept looking.

One day in late 2012, as Kim was talking to a family friend and lamenting the gauntlet of medical rabbit holes that she had explored, her friend mentioned a holistic treatment facility in Wichita, Kansas called the Hansa Center for Optimum Health. In years past, the Hansa Center had demonstrated a certain amount of success treating patients with diseases that traditional medicine wasn't helping. One of her personal friends had been effectively treated at the Hansa Center. So, after hearing that testimonial, Kim decided to do some research and reach out to the center by email.

Kim's research convinced her that the Hansa Center could help Allan—not *cure* him, but *help* him. After hearing what his mom had to say and doing his own research, Allan agreed. There was just one problem: money. The Hansa Center practiced alternative medicine, so it wasn't covered by insurance. And it was expensive. A two-week stay there would cost around $20,000 out of pocket—$20,000 that neither Allan nor his family had.

Kim had done her part. Now, Allan felt it was *his* turn to roll up his sleeves and get to work. Over the past few years, he had been doing something he does *very* well—making new friends. During his medical roller coaster ride, Allan had made connections with several local firefighters, and he even made some friends at the Apple Valley Town Hall.

So, after explaining to his fire-fighter buddy that he needed to do a fundraiser, his friend got to work. He reached out to one of his best friends, Tom Carpino, owner of one of the most successful restaurants in town. Mama Carpino's Italian Restaurant was a well-known destination for terrific, authentic homemade pasta dishes, pizza and gelato. And when Tom Carpino heard about Allan's disease and his dream of walking again, he was all in.

Tom met with Allan and decided to carve out a few hours one evening to do a one-of-a-kind fundraising dinner for Allan. He would create a special menu for the evening, Allan could sell tickets for $20 each, and ALL proceeds would go directly to Allan to fund his trip to the Hansa Center. The plan sounded delicious! So, the date was set, and Allan, his family and friends helped spread the word and sell tickets around the community.

On the night of the fundraiser, the parking lot was packed. Well over a hundred people from the community poured into the Italian eatery to enjoy a tasty dinner and support Allan. At the fundraiser, Allan's family sold custom-made "Help Allan Walk

Again" bracelets, and Allan was able to do what, up to this point, he had only done a few times—be a motivational speaker. Allan's face beamed as he shared from his heart the deep appreciation and joy he felt in that moment. To be supported by so many of his family and friends—and even perfect strangers—meant the world to him.

Allan's friends and neighbors *were* motivated. Hearts were touched. And those who attended responded with an unexpected level of generosity. The waiters and waitresses were so moved by Allan's story that they pooled their tips at the end of the night and gave them all to Allan. After the donations were counted, Allan was speechless. Not only had he raised enough money to undergo treatment at the Hansa Center, he also had enough for his new girlfriend Brittney to travel to Wichita with him for moral support.

So, it was a done deal. With his stomach full and his heart even fuller, Allan was headed to the Hansa Center.

CHAPTER 13

THE HANSA CENTER

"Then Peter said, 'Silver or gold I do not have, but what I have I give you. In the name of Jesus Christ of Nazareth, walk.'"
- Acts 3:6

From all that Allan had learned about the Hansa Center, he knew the doctors and nurses who worked there were top-notch. He'd read plenty of testimonials from patients who raved about how skilled and compassionate the staff was. Most patients dealing with chronic pain experienced a significant reduction in their pain levels. Many patients with chronic illnesses saw their symptoms disappear. And more than a few of them described the treatments as "a miracle."

So, as Allan and Brittney boarded their plane and began their three-hour flight to Wichita, Kansas, Allan was more positive than usual. As he thought about the course of events over the past few months, he couldn't help but see that God had been working all things together for his good. It certainly wasn't a coincidence that Kim's friend had told her about the Hansa Center. It was no accident that Allan's fire fighter buddy was good friends with Tom Carpino. And it was definitely no accident that the entire cost of Allan's trip had been covered by donations. So, Allan was convinced: Even though his miracle hadn't arrived signed, sealed and delivered in Baltimore or Zwickau, it was about to arrive in Wichita. He just *knew* it.

After Allan and Brittney's plane touched down in Wichita, they met up with Joe, Kim and Shavaun. Since Joe and Kim couldn't find a pet sitter to care for their four rowdy dogs, they had decided to drive their travel trailer to Kansas with the canines in tow. With three adults, four big dogs and everyone's luggage crammed into the SUV, Allan's family rolled into Wichita later that day tired and hungry, but none the worse for wear. Everyone had high hopes for what the next day would bring.

The following morning, Joe wheeled Allan into the Hansa Center. Allan was visibly nervous. His hands were sweaty, and his fidgeting was more pronounced than usual. But at the same time, he was excited to meet the doctors and nurses who would be devoting so much time to him for the next seven days. Over the past seven years, Allan had experienced his fair share of ill-tempered doctors and nurses who had the bedside manner of a Tasmanian devil.

But after only a few minutes at the Hansa Center, Allan could tell—this place was different. It wasn't just the warm, homey décor or the ultra-clean rooms. From day one, the staff and nurses didn't disappoint—especially Dr. Jernigan. Allan was beyond thrilled to learn that Dr. Jernigan was a Christian. And he wasn't just a Christian in name only. He was one of the most friendly, caring doctors that Allan had ever met.

Dr. Jernigan and his staff put Allan and his parents at ease. They were so down-to-earth. They didn't use medical jargon to make their patients feel like uneducated fools. They spoke in plain English, and their treatment philosophy, well ... it just made sense. For starters, none of their treatments involved any kind of invasive surgery. That by itself was music to Allan's ears. After all, he had already had several back surgeries that didn't offer him the long-term relief he had been promised.

Allan and his family were especially excited to hear that the

Hansa staff believed in working with God's natural design of the body—empowering the body to heal itself. Dr. Jernigan said, "Health in a bottle is a myth. If you must continually take a pill, it isn't correcting what is necessary for your body to heal." Allan and his parents all agreed: This philosophy of healing was not only biblical, it was also logical.

On Allan's first day of treatment, he met a woman who had come to the Hansa Center with a severe case of Lyme disease. She had arrived in a wheelchair but was leaving on her own two feet. As she shared her success story with Allan, his hopes skyrocketed. He was bound and determined to be the Hansa Center's next success story—the twenty-five-year-old man who was *wheeled* in but just seven days later *walked* out.

After two or three days, Allan experienced his first small miracle: His neck muscles began to relax, and the range of motion in his neck improved dramatically. As he moved his head from side to side, Allan was elated. His neck hadn't felt *that* good in a *long* time! It was an amazing first step, and Allan couldn't wait for his back to feel just as good as his neck.

Unfortunately, *that* miracle was much more elusive. By the end of the week, Allan's back hadn't shown *any* improvement. Allan was deeply disappointed, but Dr. Jernigan still had hope. He said he wanted to try some different treatments and supplements if Allan could stay for one more week. Although it hadn't been part of their original plan, after talking it over, Allan and his family decided to hang in there for another seven days. And they were beyond grateful that the proceeds from Allan's fundraiser were sufficient to cover the extra costs. After all, Dr. Jernigan was still Allan's best shot at walking again. And, truth be told, Allan and his family were in no hurry to rush home. Over the past week they had fallen in love with Kansas. Both at the clinic and in town the people were so kind and hospitable. No "Big, fat, white American pigs!" comments were heard in *that* town.

One day during Allan's second week in Kansas, he and his family took a drive through Wichita. As they were soaking in the scenery and dreaming of a simpler, quieter life, they passed by a church. Unbeknownst to his family, Allan closed his eyes and said a silent prayer, asking God to show him a sign if He wanted him to get better and walk again. His eyes became misty as he prayed, "God, if You want me to stay in a wheelchair and not be healed, show me. As hard as it would be to *not* get better, just show me, and I'll be okay with that."

As soon as Allan spoke those words in prayer, he felt an unmistakable sensation—something like an electrical impulse—radiating through his back and legs. His legs felt a sudden rush of strength, like Popeye the Sailor Man downing a can of spinach. The pain in his back decreased significantly. Allan's tear ducts burst forth. He just couldn't ... stop ... crying. His parents and sister noticed that Allan was bordering on hysterical, so they asked him, "Allan, what's wrong?" He struggled to explain that they were "happy tears," not sad ones, but he found it difficult to speak. He felt so relieved and so excited. He just couldn't talk.

But finally, he composed himself enough to say, "Mom, stop the car!" Kim quickly pulled over to the side of the road, and her jaw nearly dropped as she heard Allan say, "I feel like God is healing me. I want to try and walk."

That's all Kim needed to hear. She flung open her door and rushed to the other side of the SUV to open Allan's door. And, holding Kim's hand for balance, Allan swung both legs out of the vehicle, placed his feet on the ground, stood upright and took a few baby steps along the roadside in front of him.

Allan and his mom collapsed into each other's arms, crying. And their tears were contagious. As Kim bawled her eyes out, Joe, Shavaun and Brittney joined right in with her. They made quite a scene on the side of the road, but they couldn't care less. They were in another world. And Allan couldn't wait to return to the Hansa Center to surprise Dr. Jernigan with his God-given miracle.

Minutes later, with Dr. Jernigan watching, Allan stood up from his wheelchair and took a few steps toward his doctor. Dr.

Jernigan's response was priceless. In stunned disbelief, he turned to Allan and said, "Oh, man! I could cry!" And he almost did, then and there.

Just a few days later, Allan and his family said their goodbyes, leaving the Hansa Center in their rearview mirror. As Allan and Brittney boarded their return flight home, they felt grateful for Allan's improvement. Without a doubt, his neck felt much better, and he was able to stand and walk without much assistance. But he couldn't shake the nagging thought: Although he had experienced two breakthrough miracles in Wichita, they were small miracles compared to the ones he had experienced at Johns Hopkins Medical Center and the Paracelsus Klinik. As Allan left the Hansa Center, he felt better and stronger than he had two weeks earlier, but he didn't feel as good or as strong as when he had left Baltimore or Germany.

So, despite the surge of strength through his legs, it appeared that God had given him His answer: At this point in time, Allan would *not* be healed, and he would *not* be able to retire his wheelchair. Sure enough, within three months of returning from the Hansa Center, Allan was back in his wheelchair. The following year, he returned to Dr. Jernigan for a reevaluation and more treatments. But this time, there was no improvement at all.

Then a follow-up email from Dr. Warnke in Germany explained why. He pointed out that arachnoiditis is a progressive disease that causes recurring inflammation around the spinal cord. Some treatments and medications could reduce the inflammation, thereby improving Allan's pain level. But, sooner or later, the inflammation would return, bringing the excruciating pain and immobility with it. Any so-called "cure" and any apparent "miracle" would be, at best, temporary. Surgery would never cure him. Medications would never heal him. Physical therapy would never rehabilitate him. Hoping for a cure was futile. It would only lead to disappointment.

And coming to grips with this reality was one of the hardest things Allan ever had to do. He began to understand more than ever why so many men and women with arachnoiditis commit suicide. Living with constant pain is extremely difficult. But living without any hope of relief from that pain—that's even harder.

So, as Allan navigated this harsh reality, he had to shift his focus from what he *couldn't* do to what he *could* do. He redirected his thoughts of being healed to fulfilling his God-given mission. Even if he would never walk again, it was time to live out his calling—a calling to "be strong and courageous," living his life for the glory of God while inspiring others to do the same. It was time for Allan, by God's grace and strength, to start building a legacy.

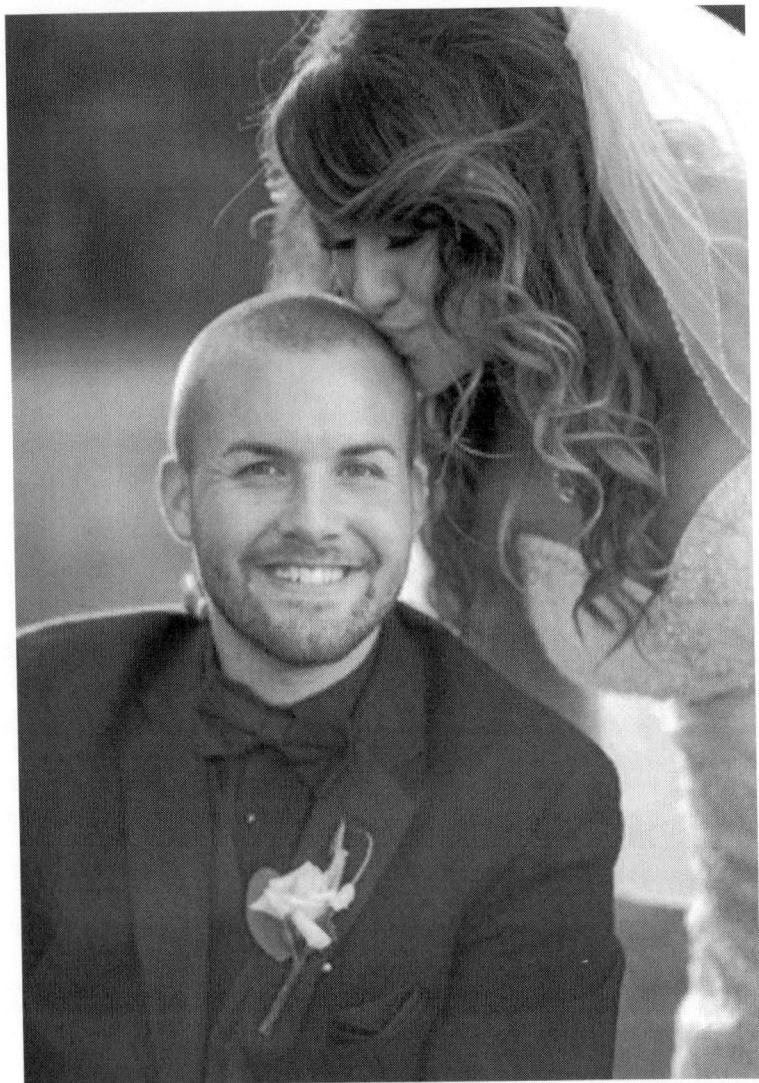

The newlyweds share a tender moment just minutes after their
wedding ceremony.

PART FOUR

BUILDING A LEGACY

Chapter 14

Love at First Sight?

*"Many women do noble things, but you surpass them all.
Charm is deceptive, and beauty is fleeting; but a
woman who fears the LORD is to be praised."*
- Proverbs 31:29-30

Since the age of seventeen, Allan's life had been Groundhog Day. Hope. Disappointment. Hope. Disappointment. Repeat.

For a young athlete like Allan, it was extremely difficult coming to terms with having a debilitating neurological disease. But it was better than the alternative—continuing to have his hopes built up only to see them crash and burn. Although Allan had long given up his dream of becoming the Dodgers' next Mike Piazza or the Lakers' next Kobe Bryant, he had certainly hoped to be able to do the *basic* activities that, seemingly, every other young man was able to do: Drive a car. Get a regular job. Shoot some hoops with his buddies. And—with a little bit of luck—dance with his bride on his wedding day, give his daughter a piggyback ride and toss the baseball at the park with his son.

But short of a miracle of biblical proportions, Allan would never be able to do *any* of these things (or dozens of others) that most young men take for granted. So, in the months following his diagnosis at Johns Hopkins in 2008, there were many nights when Allan lay awake in bed with a whirlwind of heavy questions swirling in his head.

What kind of girl would ever want to date *him*? What could he possibly offer her that a thousand other guys couldn't? How could he meet her needs? How could he earn an income? What if the doctors were right—that he would most likely *never* be able to have children? And even if a one-in-a-million girl *was* willing to date him and eventually marry him, could he, in good conscience, go through with it? Wouldn't it be unfair to expect *any* girl to be not just his wife but also his full-time chauffeur and part-time nurse? These were heart-wrenching questions for Allan to ask and work through. But he soon discovered that God didn't want him to work through them on his own.

Enter ... Brittney Hernandez. Allan and Brittney had attended Apple Valley Christian School together. Although Brittney was just a sophomore during Allan's senior year, they *did* have a math class together. In fact, their assigned seats were side by side. On more than one occasion Brittney helped Allan figure out a math problem that had him stumped. But other than that, they didn't interact much. They didn't socialize with the same group of friends. Truth be told, they didn't give each other a passing thought outside of class. So, after Allan's graduation, they fell out of contact. Out of sight, out of mind.

But that all changed the year Allan headed for Germany. In early 2009, Joe and Kim threw a big "Sweet 16" birthday party for Shavaun, and one of her friends invited nineteen-year-old Brittney to attend. As Brittney walked through the front door of the Schwartz home, she was surprised to see Allan in a wheelchair, being pushed by their family friend Erika.

Allan and his good friend Garret wasted no time informing Brittney and her friends that the two of them were the official "bouncers" at the party. At the first sign of any funny business, they were ready to steamroll any troublemakers with his wheelchair. Brittney laughed, but her mind was racing. She immediately recognized Allan as the graduating senior who had sat next to her in math class three years earlier, but she couldn't tell if he remembered her. So, she settled for a quick "Hi!" before making her way to the birthday girl.

A little while later, Brittney saw Allan in the kitchen with his friends. He was eating, laughing and, quite obviously, having a great time. But throughout the evening, a question kept nagging her: *Why was Allan in that wheelchair?* Just three years earlier, he had played every sport that AVCS offered. But now he seemed at home in a wheelchair. Why? He didn't appear to have any kind of debilitating injury. No leg brace. No cast. No signs of paralysis. He looked perfectly healthy. She just *had* to know what happened.

Brittney discretely asked a few of her friends, but they seemed just as surprised as she was. They didn't have any answers. So, not being one to leave a mystery unsolved, Brittney did a little research that weekend. She scoured the internet—especially Facebook—looking for clues. Certainly, a 20-year-old social butterfly like Allan was on Facebook. But to her surprise, her search turned up empty. The mystery continued to gnaw at her, but she didn't want to come across as nosy, so she left well enough alone and moved on with her post-graduation life.

Until August. As Brittney was scrolling through Facebook, Allan's name popped up. It turned out he wasn't a stranger to social media after all. She quickly sent him a friend request and was thrilled to see that within a short time he accepted it.

Within a week, the texting began—first on Facebook Messenger and then by phone. Brittney mustered the courage to ask Allan about his wheelchair, and, to her surprise, he shared his story without hesitation. Each of them found the other so easy to talk to. Their conversations flowed effortlessly.

So much had changed in Allan's life since his baby sister's "Sweet 16" party five months earlier. Two months after the party, Allan had flown to Germany for his life-changing surgery. So, as

Allan and Brittney texted and chatted on the phone, they had plenty to talk about. Allan had a new lease on life. With minimal pain, he could stand, walk, exercise, lift weights and do dozens of other physical activities he hadn't been able to do in several years. He couldn't wait to tell Brittney all about it. And she couldn't wait to *hear* all about it. To her, Allan's story was nothing short of *amazing!*

One evening in September, Allan reached out to Brittney and asked her if they could grab a cup of coffee together—ASAP. At the time, Joe and Kim were going through a rough patch in their marriage. Allan explained that he just needed to get away from the tension and breathe some fresh air. Since Brittney didn't have any plans, she said, "Sure!" Within a few minutes she was in Allan's driveway. He hopped in the car, and together they headed to The Grind coffee shop in Apple Valley.

Allan and Brittney expected to be there for an hour or two. But before they knew it, two hours turned into four or five. They talked and laughed. Laughed and talked. Finally, one of the baristas walked over to their table and told them, "I'm sorry. We're closing now. You'll have to leave." That bad news would have squashed most conversations, but not Allan and Brittney's. Since they weren't done talking, they decided to continue their "date" across the parking lot at Del Taco. And they pushed the limits of Del Taco's operating hours as well.

As they sat across the table from each other, Allan was an open book—sharing details of his journey that he'd never shared with anyone else. He walked her through the two years of failed treatments, ineffective medications and misdiagnoses. He shared with her the relief and fear he felt when he finally received his diagnosis at Johns Hopkins and how that five-day hospital visit turned into more than five weeks. He enthusiastically shared the details of how his mom had discovered Dr. Warnke and how his spinal surgery had been an answer to prayer.

Brittney listened in amazement. She couldn't fully wrap her mind around the fact that such a young man had dealt with so much suffering in his life, yet he had such a positive outlook. Allan was walking at a normal pace. He was sitting, standing and scooting into a booth like any normal man. No casual observer would *ever* believe Allan had a life-threatening, debilitating disease that, until recently, had confined him to a wheelchair.

As Allan shared his story with Brittney, she experienced the full gamut of emotions. Her heart ached as he walked her through his pain and disappointments. And she rejoiced as he shared God's answers to prayer—especially the miracle in Zwickau. Never in her life had Brittney met a man like Allan. On the drive home that night she thought to herself, *That guy is something special. There's something different about him.*

After Brittney dropped him off at home, Allan floated through his front door. In that moment he wasn't worried about his parents' marriage or focused on the tension in the house. He was in a different world. Despite being tired, he couldn't stop smiling. He thought, *That girl is amazing, and so pretty! She's so easy to talk to. Thank You, God, for this evening I just had.*

Sleep was hard to come by that night, but Allan eventually drifted off with one prevailing thought racing through his head: *No matter what else I have going on tomorrow, I HAVE to see Brittney again.*

After a not-so-good night's sleep, Allan reached out to his new heartthrob the following morning and asked her if she would like to get together again. Not surprisingly, she said, "Yes!" They picked up right where they'd left off the night before—laughing and talking for hours.

After the third day of spending time together, Allan got up the nerve to call Brittney on the phone and tell her—rather awkwardly—"I really like you ... but not as just a friend." Brittney tried to cover the awkwardness with a giggle. She responded in the only way that made sense to her at the time, "Oh! Well, thanks." (She figured she might as well play hard to get.)

Brittney obviously wasn't scared off by Allan's frankness, because their daily communication continued. Phone calls. Texts.

Dates. And on September 21st, Allan took Brittney on a very special date to Huntington Beach. They enjoyed a pepperoni pizza at one of Allan's favorite restaurants, BJ's Pizza and Brewery. And at sunset, they walked barefoot down the beach.

The evening was going just as Allan had imagined it. They felt the cool sand beneath their feet, heard the waves crashing gently beside them and admired the beauty of the horizon glowing in beautiful hues of yellow and orange. Allan tried to play it cool, but Brittney knew what was on his mind. It was blatantly obvious —he was getting ready to plant one on her.

With sweaty palms and a racing heart, Allan leaned in for a kiss, and OUCH! He was denied. Brittney, who calls herself "The Queen of Stalling," looked into Allan's disappointed eyes and said, "Can you just hold me?"

Well, Allan thought, *I didn't drive all this way for a hug. But if a hug is what this beautiful girl wants, a hug is what I'll give her.* So, Allan and Brittney held each other as the waves slid gently over their feet.

And at long last, the perfect moment came. Allan leaned in, and this time, Brittney didn't hold up a stop sign. As the sun disappeared beyond the horizon, Allan and Brittney shared their first kiss, and it was, in Brittney's words, "Perfect!"

On the drive home, Southern California's newest couple was listening to Christian music on the radio, and Hillsong's hit worship song "Hosanna" began playing. As Brittney drove down the freeway, still savoring the sweet moment she and Allan had just enjoyed on the beach, she heard a ghastly sound coming from the passenger's seat next to her. It sounded like someone was in terrible pain. As she glanced to her right in alarm, she couldn't believe her eyes. Allan was smiling, eyes closed, as he lifted his hands and sang his heart out:

I see a generation
Rising up to take their place
With selfless faith, with selfless faith

I see a near revival
Stirring as we pray and seek
We're on our knees, we're on our knees

Hosanna, Hosanna
Hosanna in the highest!

Heal my heart and make it clean
Open up my eyes to the things unseen
Show me how to love like You have loved me
Break my heart for what breaks Yours
Everything I am for Your kingdom's cause
As I walk from earth into eternity

Although Brittney's ears felt assaulted by the crooning of her cute date—who obviously couldn't carry a tune in a bucket—it was, strangely, one of the most beautiful sounds she'd ever heard. It was authentic, passionate worship resonating from the lips of a man who had been to hell and back and understood the mercy and grace of God better than most Christians twice his age. Tears slipped down her cheeks as Brittney glanced over at the Christ-loving young man she'd just kissed. She felt the presence of God in her car. No vision. No audible voice. But she knew He was there. Brittney grabbed Allan's hand and began singing along in worship with him. And as she did, she could almost hear God whispering, "Brittney, he's the one for you. He's the one."

CHAPTER 15

MY GIRL!

*"The LORD God said, 'It is not good for the man
to be alone. I will make a helper suitable for him.'"*
- Genesis 2:18

It only took Allan a little over a week to officially ask Brittney the big question: "Will you be my girlfriend?" In typical Allan fashion, it was a little corny. But at the same time, it was sincere and heartfelt. Brittney responded with a nervous giggle and a "Yes! Of course, I will!"

After all, it was becoming more and more clear that Allan was the man of her dreams. And he had been so sweet that afternoon. A dozen red roses. Video games and air hockey at Dave and Buster's. And a delicious steak dinner at Yard House. It was another date that was, in both their minds ... "perfect."

But *perfect* usually doesn't last. Honeymoons come to an end, and we eventually wake up from our dreams. Just three weeks after their big date at Dave and Buster's, Brittney and Shavaun joined Allan for one of his all-time-favorite activities—singing his heart out at a Christian concert. The Christian rock group Skillet was performing in Los Angeles, and Allan couldn't miss the chance to be there. So, on October 23, 2009, Allan—with two brunette beauties at his side—stood in the concert hall with the biggest Cheshire-Cat smile on his face. The concert was *so* loud, Brittney couldn't hear a single word Shavaun was screaming in her ear. But her hand gestures got the message across: *Take a look at my brother.* So, they both turned and looked at Allan, singing and dancing like it was 1999.

But it didn't last. Early in the concert Allan turned to Brittney and said, "Something feels weird in my back." She didn't know what that meant, but Allan felt it best to sit down for a little while. So, he did. Down and back up. Down and back up. So went the next two hours.

At one point Allan sat on a bench outside the concert hall holding his face in his hands and crying out to God in prayer. Panic swept over him as he began to consider a worst-case scenario: Arachnoiditis was back with a vengeance. His pain was back for good.

By the end of the concert, Brittney and Shavaun had grown worried as well. They asked Allan how he was feeling. He didn't want to worry them, so he left it at, "Something just doesn't feel right." Without a doubt, there was a heaviness in the air on the drive home to Apple Valley. As Allan kissed Brittney goodnight, he told her he'd probably feel better in the morning. Maybe he'd just overexerted himself at the concert. Standing up too long. Dancing too hard. Unexpectedly straining a muscle in his back.

Brittney texted Allan first thing the next morning. She had been thinking about him and praying for him off and on throughout the night, hoping for the best.

But Allan's answers to her questions weren't the good news she'd hoped for. "Yeah. My back still hurts a little, but I'm going to be okay." Brittney wasn't convinced, but she tried to avoid thoughts of doom and gloom. After all, Allan knew his disease and its symptoms better than she did. Perhaps he was right. Maybe it was nothing to worry about.

But it definitely wasn't "nothing." As the days passed, Allan's pain slithered down his spine and legs like an unwelcome serpent.

Walking became more painful. And his daily routines became more tedious. With each passing day, Allan could feel his body deteriorating. It felt like every day his body was aging ten years.

It became more and more difficult for Brittney to watch Allan grimace in pain as he did his best to shuffle across the room. She urged him to use his wheelchair, but at first, he stubbornly refused. He feared that if he returned to his wheelchair, he would be kissing his walking goodbye. And to him, the stakes seemed higher than ever. Brittney wouldn't want to date a guy in a wheel-chair, would she? She wouldn't want to be the one to lug his chair in and out of her car or push him around everywhere they went. Once again, the doubts swirled in Allan's head as he thought, *She didn't sign up for this!*

But despite his best efforts to remain on his feet, Allan eventu-ally cried "Uncle!" and returned to his life on wheels. Part of him *hated* that wheelchair. But he knew he needed it. So, he wiped off about eight months of accumulated dust and reluctantly took a seat. And in her wisdom, Brittney didn't waste any time addressing the elephant in the room. She told Allan in no uncer-tain terms, "When I said 'Yes!' to being your girlfriend, I didn't see this coming. But I don't see you any differently. No matter how bad it gets ... I'm not going anywhere."

In the weeks that followed, Kim kicked into high gear to schedule the MRIs and calls to Baltimore and Germany, but this time Brittney rolled up her sleeves to help in any way she could. She helped with the research. She helped tend to Allan as needed. And, most importantly, she kept Allan's spirits up.

His heart ached as he watched the girl he loved do the heavy lifting with his wheelchair. He seemed to constantly be saying, "I'm sorry." "I'm sorry I can't open the car door for you." "I'm sorry I can't put the wheelchair in the trunk for you." "I'm sorry you have to drive all the time." But Brittney didn't mind. She knew that any inconvenience she dealt with was minor compared to the pain Allan endured every day. In fact, Allan's concern for her small inconveniences just made her love him even more.

As 2010 faded into 2011, and 2011 faded into 2012, Brittney fielded many questions from her friends and family members who were both curious and concerned about her relationship with Allan. More than once, friends asked her, "How are you able to handle seeing him in pain?" Brittney's response was wise beyond her years: "I don't see him in pain. I see Allan as a man who desires and loves God. I see his selfless acts. I see his drive. I see his respect for me and others. And I don't ask myself, 'Should I help him?' I just *help* him."

Brittney's parents asked her to picture what her life would look like if she and Allan got married. Respectfully, Brittney explained, "As I see it, my part in our relationship is easy. Allan's part is much harder. He's the one in pain. He's the one who's had to overcome so many disappointments. Anyone who meets him can see that his heart is so real and genuine. He loves God *so* much, and he loves me more than anyone else could. I would feel honored to be his wife."

CHAPTER 16

WEDDING BELLS

*"He who finds a wife finds what is good
and receives favor from the Lord."*
- Proverbs 18:22

From 2011 to 2013, Brittney had a front-row seat for many of Allan's treatment successes and failures: the IV treatments, Hyperbaric Chamber Therapy, acupuncture and his go-for-broke trip to the Hansa Center. Brittney was right there for the emotional times of prayer. She was on the scene for Allan's fundraiser and motivational speech at Mama Carpino's. She didn't just witness his dashed hopes and shattered dreams ... she *lived* it. And through it all, she didn't waver. Her love for Allan grew deeper—as did Allan's love for Brittney.

So, Brittney and her family fully expected that, sooner or later, Allan would pop the question. And he did on November 23, 2013. After asking Brittney's parents for her hand in marriage and getting their blessing, Allan asked Brittney if she'd like to join him at the Yard House in Rancho Cucamonga to have lunch with his buddy Matt and his new girlfriend. Of course, it was just a ploy to get Brittney back to the restaurant where he had asked her to be his girlfriend four years earlier. She had said, "Yes!" back then. *Maybe*, Allan thought, *she'll say "Yes!" again.* With a little bit of luck, he had a good chance of batting a thousand with his home field advantage at Yard House.

After arriving at the restaurant and being seated at a booth overlooking the courtyard, Allan excused himself to "use the bathroom." After a minute or two, Allan and Brittney's favorite song started playing. Brittney thought, *What a coincidence! It's too bad Allan is missing it.* She wanted to point it out to Allan, but she was afraid it would be over before he got back.

As she nervously waited for Allan to return from his pit stop, out of the corner of her eye she saw someone standing outside the window next to her table. As Brittney turned to get a closer look, she was surprised to see one of her best friends standing on the other side of the glass holding up an 8 ½ x 11 sheet of white paper with a typed note that read, "You being a part of my life has made these four years the best of my life." After a few seconds, she dropped the piece of paper, turned and walked away.

Brittney thought that was strange ... but not as strange as what happened a few seconds later. Up walked another friend with a sheet of paper pressed to the glass. This one read, "I asked for the Lord to bless me with a woman of God, and He gave me more. He gave me an angel." In the same way, that friend dropped her note, turned and walked away. One by one, other friends and family members stepped up to the window and held up sheets of paper.

"You are my rock and my backbone. I thank God every day for you."

"As each day goes by, I love you more and more."

"I am so blessed to not only call you my girlfriend but my best friend."

"I want to ask you to officially start another journey and chapter with me here today."

"This will be the best memory of our relationship so far."

As the tears rolled down Brittney's cheeks, Joe and Kim stepped up to the window holding two sheets of paper that read, "I have an important question to ask you. A question you will always remember and will change our lives forever." As they turned and walked away, up walked Brittney's parents, with two final sheets of paper from Allan: "Will you make me the luckiest guy in the world?"

As Brittney's parents turned and walked away, Allan rolled up to Brittney's table in his powerchair holding one final written message: "Will you marry me?" As he held up his piece of paper for Brittney, she burst out, "Absolutely!"

At that moment Allan gripped the armrests of his wheelchair with both hands and rose to his feet for one of the most meaningful hugs he and Brittney had ever shared. And as they stood next to their table holding each other tightly, the restaurant erupted in applause—led by Allan and Brittney's family and friends who, meanwhile, had gathered just a few feet behind where Brittney had been sitting.

It was one of the best days of Allan and Brittney's lives, and it was all caught on video. Allan had hired a videographer to record all the key scenes: Brittney waiting at the table, the notes at the window, Allan's official proposal, even a post-proposal interview with Allan and Brittney. And when the final edits were complete, Allan posted the video on YouTube, where it can still be viewed today. Allan labeled it "Best Wedding Proposal Ever! Brittney and Allan." Sure, it's a matter of opinion. But it very well *could* be the best wedding proposal ever.

THE BIG DAY

In the months that followed, Allan and Brittney dreamed and planned, planned and dreamed. They wanted their wedding to be extra special, just as their marriage would be. They settled on a date and location: March 20, 2015 at the Green River Country Club in Corona, California. The grounds were perfect for both their wedding ceremony and their photos. And the banquet hall, with its gorgeous views of the golf course, was ideal for their reception. As an added bonus, the cart paths around the clubhouse and property made it easy for him to get anywhere he wanted to go in his trusty powerchair.

On the morning of the wedding, Brittney was beyond excited. And, surprisingly, she wasn't very nervous ... until she started getting dressed. Allan, on the other hand, had butterflies from the very moment he woke up. His thoughts raced a mile a minute. *Will everyone make it to the country club on time? Will there be a lot of traffic on a Friday night? Will I remember what to say at the altar? Where is my tux? Who has the ring?*

Allan and Brittney decided not to see each other before the ceremony, but it was easier said than done—especially when the 4 p.m. ceremony was delayed by an hour. But one of the most special moments of the day happened just minutes before the ceremony. Allan rode his powerchair up to the end of a wall in the reception hall, while Brittney stood on the other side of the wall. They extended their arms and held hands as Allan led them both in a prayer.

Minutes later, Allan rode his powerchair up the center aisle to the front of the outdoor wedding venue. As the time came for the ceremony to begin, Allan looked down the aisle and laid his eyes on the most beautiful girl he had ever seen. Brittney's face glowed as she walked up the aisle in her traditional, floor-length white wedding dress. Her parents both escorted her—her dad on her right arm and her mom on her left.

And when Brittney saw Allan for the first time, her eyes fixed on him alone. She barely noticed the other 120 people huddled on both sides of the aisle. She thought Allan looked so handsome in his black tux, waiting for her up front. She couldn't wait to spend the rest of her life at her best friend's side. She and Allan both knew there would be plenty of tough times ahead. But they also knew in their hearts that God had put them together for a much bigger purpose than they could imagine.

Full disclosure: As the pastor of Allan's home church, I had the privilege of officiating the wedding. During the ceremony, I shared a conversation I'd had with Allan and Brittney during their pre-marital counseling a few weeks earlier. I asked them this question: "What one word would you like used to describe your marriage in fifty years?" After giving it some thought and discussion, they had chosen a word that most engaged couples wouldn't choose. Most couples I've met with choose words like "happy," "united" or "in love." But Allan and Brittney chose the word … "godly." More than anything else, Allan and Brittney wanted their marriage to honor God and reflect His character.

As the ceremony continued, I quoted one of Allan's favorite Bible verses: Jeremiah 29:11, "'For I know the plans I have for you,' declares the LORD, 'plans to prosper you and not to harm you, plans to give you hope and a future.'" Then I shared a personal message God had laid on my heart for this very special couple:

> Allan, I know this verse has been an encouragement to you over the past eight years as you've battled your disease. As you've experienced level-10 pain on a regular basis, your faith has been strengthened as you read and memorized this verse—convinced that even though your circumstances and your pain don't make sense, God is *somehow* at work for the good. He is somehow prospering you and not harming you. Somehow, He is weaving your pain and suffering into His master plan, and even though you may not understand it now, He *will* bring you hope and a future.

Despite the challenges you will face, despite the pain and heartache and frustration, you must both hold tight to God's promise that He is at work for the good, prospering you and not harming you, giving you hope and a future.

Allan and Brittney, I also want to share something else that I believe the Lord put on my heart to share with you. Many married couples your age are able to blend in with other married couples and slip under people's radar. You two *won't* have that luxury. Allan, because you are in that wheelchair dealing with a rare neurological disease, whether you like it or not, people will be watching you, both of you. People aren't used to seeing a 26-year-old husband in a wheelchair. And people aren't used to seeing a committed young wife patiently and lovingly caring for her 26-year husband in a wheelchair. Don't ever forget: People are watching you, so don't mess it up.

Allan and Brittney, God has given you both a wonderful gift: the gift of influence. Allan, we continue to hope and pray for you to one day be healed of your arachnoiditis once and for all. But in the meantime, you two have been given a God-given opportunity to show a world that's watching what uncondi-tional love looks like in a marriage that deals with physical pain and suffering every day. You two have the opportunity to demonstrate what mutual respect, self-sacrifice, compassion and joy look like in a marriage that faces a unique set of chal-lenges. You two will be able to show a watching world that if Jesus Christ is in a marriage, you can do all things through Christ who strengthens you. What a privilege! What a wonderful opportunity you both have to show the world how wonderful marriage can be when it's godly.

Afterward, Allan and Brittney did their best to hold back their tears as they exchanged their vows: "I promise before God and these witnesses to be your loving and faithful husband/wife.

To be true to you in sickness and in health, in joy and in sorrow, in plenty and in want. And forsaking all others, I will keep myself to you and to you only, cherishing and respecting you as long as we both live."

A few minutes later, the ceremony came to a close, and I was honored to speak the words Allan had been waiting for over five years to hear: "Allan, you may kiss your beautiful bride." Most grooms in that situation waste no time going in for the kill. But Allan wasn't "most grooms." There was hardly a dry eye on the lawn as everyone witnessed something they had never seen at a wedding.

Allan braced himself on the armrests of his powerchair and slowly stood up. And despite the intense pain shooting up and down his back and legs, he leaned forward and gave Brittney a tender kiss. His back and legs were screaming in agony, but he refused to allow them to rob him and his bride of that once-in-a-lifetime moment. But once that moment was over, Allan succumbed to the pain and quickly sat back down.

To everyone's surprise, Allan stood up two more times that evening—during his "first dance" with Brittney and once more, for about thirty seconds, during the mother-son dance. For the better part of nine years, Kim had been Allan's number one health advocate—spending countless hours on the internet, on the phone and in dozens of doctors' offices, testing facilities and hospitals, fighting for her son's health. Allan was where he was on his wedding day in large part because of his mother, and he knew it. So, on his wedding day he gave her the greatest "thank you" gift he could ever give her: He rose to his feet one last time ... this time for his mom.

Some would say Allan and Brittney's marriage was off to a fairy-tale start. Like most young couples, they didn't know the half of the challenges and difficulties they would face in years to come, but they had a much clearer picture than most. Together, they had experienced much more pain, heartache, and disappointment than any other young couple they knew. And through it all, they had chosen faith, hope and love ... together.

At their wedding reception, as Allan stood on the dance floor just a few inches in front of his powerchair, holding Brittney in his arms, the eyes of their family and friends were fastened on them. Everyone in the room knew they were witnessing something special ... *very* special. Allan and Brittney were unlike any couple they'd ever seen, and it wasn't *just* because of Allan's wheelchair. They were a living illustration of 1 Corinthians 13:13: "Now these three remain: faith, hope and love. But the greatest of these is love."

CHAPTER 17

TWO LITTLE MIRACLES

*"Children are a heritage from the LORD, offspring
a reward from Him. Like arrows in the hands
of a warrior are the children born in one's youth.
Blessed is the man whose quiver is full of them."*
- Psalm 127:3-5

Allan and Brittney's wedding day was hands-down one of the best days of their lives. And their wedding night was the icing on the cake. It was a night they had anxiously anticipated and patiently waited for. For well over a year, they hadn't just *talked* about keeping God at the center of their engagement; they had disciplined themselves to *keep* Him there by waiting for each other until their wedding night. And that made their first night together as husband and wife extra special.

The next day, Allan and Brittney boarded their plane at LAX and made their way to the Excellence Playa Mujeres resort in Cancun, Mexico. Although flying coach wreaked havoc on Allan's back and legs, on the other end of the flight, they were greeted with seven swimming pools, all-inclusive food and drinks, and a powdery white sand beach. It was the perfect setting for their first romantic getaway as husband and wife. There wasn't a single Wienerschnizel or Yard House within a thousand miles of the resort, but even Allan had to admit—the food was pretty amazing.

And the sunsets were gorgeous. Photos couldn't begin to do them justice. The divine mixture of oranges, yellows and purples in the evening sky were, in Allan's words, "breathtaking!" The vistas were heavenly, and Allan soaked it in much more than most men his age would have. He had learned to appreciate life's small blessings and feast his eyes on the beauty of God's creation. So, as the week unfolded, Allan found himself in a constant state of praise and worship. He echoed King David, who proclaimed in Psalm 19:1-2: "The heavens declare the glory of God, and the skies proclaim the work of His hands. Day after day they pour forth speech; night after night they display knowledge."

As Allan sat in his reclining beach chair next to his pretty bride, looking across the sparkling blue Caribbean, his mind raced with thoughts of the long path he had traveled. It had been nine years since he had first felt the sensation of crippling pain in his lower back. In hindsight, it all seemed surreal. As a teenager, he never would have imagined the ordeal that awaited him.

No one in their right mind would have denied that Allan's past nine years had been a living nightmare. But strangely, at age 26, he was the happiest newlywed on earth. As he sat there, he wanted to pinch himself. His life in that moment seemed too good to be true.

Sure, he had faced indescribable pain, but that pain hadn't beaten him. No doubt, he had questioned and even doubted God's purpose and plan, but his faith was stronger than ever. Of course, there had been many days when he hated arachnoiditis with a passion, but at the same time, his disease had proved itself to be an uninvited friend who had helped shape Allan into a much stronger Christian than he would have been otherwise.

So, if arachnoiditis had somehow helped pave the way for him to be worshiping Jesus Christ in paradise with the woman of his dreams at his side, arachnoiditis was a gift from God. "The Lord gave, and the LORD has taken away; may the name of the LORD be praised" (Job 1:21).

Even as Allan fidgeted and shifted his lower body to find a position that best quieted the pain in his back and legs, he felt the strange, unexpected peace of God that transcends understanding. In that moment he was deeply grateful to be alive, thankful for the breath in his lungs and in awe of the love he felt from his Lord and Savior Jesus Christ. So, there on that beach, Allan made a vow to enjoy every moment of every day that God would give him, regardless of whether or not those moments were laced with pain.

In that slice of paradise, Allan and Brittney spent some invaluable one-on-one time discussing the journey they were on together ... past, present and future. In the months leading up to their wedding day, they had many conversations about what their new family would look like in years to come. Both Allan and Brittney wanted to have children, but they knew the odds were against them. Brittney had heard with her own ears what Dr. Jernigan had told Allan at the Hansa Center: His low testosterone levels and autoimmune abnormalities would make it very difficult for Allan to get his wife pregnant. And as grim as it sounded, Dr. Jernigan's assessment was more hopeful than that of the other doctors who had evaluated Allan. Many of them had told Allan flat out, "You will NEVER be able to have kids."

So, Allan and Brittney decided to do their part as a married couple to pave the way for pregnancy but, ultimately, to leave the results up to God. Since they both desired to *have* children, they *prayed* for children. But they trusted God to have the final say. If God answered their prayers with a "No," that would be difficult to stomach, but they were determined to trust His will. After all, they agreed, His ways were higher than their ways; His thoughts were higher than their thoughts, and His plans for their family were so much better than their own plans. So, Allan and Brittney put their childbearing squarely in God's hands. They were both convinced that if God allowed them to have children at some point down the road, He would know exactly what they could and couldn't handle, and His timing would be perfect.

Allan and Brittney's honeymoon lasted far longer than their one-week trip to Cancun. Their first few months of marriage were filled with wonderful times of conversation, laughter, prayer, worship, day trips and family gatherings. And each month as they "tried to get pregnant," they continued to trust God. But Brittney secretly wondered if their attempts to get pregnant were all for nothing—an exercise in futility.

But her worries were answered in an instant when she took a pregnancy test six months into their marriage. The little pink line didn't lie. She was pregnant! Brittney couldn't believe her eyes. She had to read the instructions on the box just to make sure she wasn't jumping to the wrong conclusion. Her cranks started turning to come up with a creative way to share the amazing news with Allan. And she thought of the perfect way. All it required was a quick trip to Target.

On September 21, 2015—the six-year anniversary of their first kiss—Brittney came home from work and handed Allan a small gift bag. He asked her, "What is this?" but she refused to give a hint. All she offered him was a subtle grin and sparkling eyes as she responded, "You'll just have to open it and see."

So, Allan pulled out the tissue paper and reached into the bag. His jaw dropped as he pulled out a Los Angeles Dodgers onesie along with Brittney's positive pregnancy test. As Allan and Brittney held each other and started crying, Allan couldn't stop shouting, "No way! I don't believe it! We're going to have a baby!" It was yet another miraculous moment on their journey that inspired Allan to erupt in a fresh chorus of praise and thanks to the God of miracles. God is good, and in that moment, Allan believed in His goodness more than ever.

Allan and Brittney were over the moon, but they didn't want to set their hopes too high. After all, miscarriages are very common early in a woman's pregnancy. So, Brittney scheduled an appointment with her OB-GYN, who determined she was in her fifth week. The ultrasound didn't show a heartbeat, so Brittney scheduled a follow-up ultrasound for the following week. And to their delight, their baby's heartbeat registered steady and strong. Their doctor-defying dream of having children was becoming a reality, but they were only *cautiously* optimistic. After all, they had experienced their fair share of bubble-bursting letdowns. And Brittney had recently had several friends lose their babies in their final months of pregnancy. One of her friends had even lost her baby boy within 48 hours of birth.

In the weeks and months that followed, Brittney's follow-up ultrasounds and ever-growing tummy slowly transformed their cautious optimism into sheer excitement and anticipation. As the time for her delivery drew closer, the chance of a miscarriage became much less likely. Their confidence was boosted every time they heard their baby's heartbeat, felt the unmistakable kicks and viewed the images on the ultrasound monitor. One of their favorite moments was viewing their baby during the 3D ultrasound. It was absolutely stunning—seeing their little one's fingers, toes, ears and nose in such crisp detail.

And that wasn't all that the ultrasound revealed in crystal clear detail. Allan and Brittney both wanted to know the gender of their baby ahead of time, so they asked their sonagram technician to go in for a closer look. The results were unmistakable— Allan and Brittney were having a boy. Their excitement grew, and they began discussing names for the soon-to-be newest member of the Schwartz family. One name rose to the top of their list: Rylen Allan. Not only did they love the name Rylen, they were proud to give him a middle name in honor of Allan's "Papa Allan" and his mom's dad "Grandpa Allan" who had passed before Allan was born.

Although there were many anxious moments along the way, Brittney's nine months of pregnancy flew by. On May 25, 2016, Allan's twenty-eighth birthday, Brittney felt that Baby Rylen was on his way. So, she and Allan grabbed the hospital bag that had already been carefully packed, and they made the short drive to St.

Mary Medical Center. Over the next twenty-four hours, they played the waiting game.

Allan and Brittney had hoped and prayed for a smooth, safe delivery. When all was said and done ... at least it was safe. Brittney wasn't able to dilate past a four, and she passed out several times during the day from the pain. Knowing how epidurals had made Allan's bad back issues even worse, she held off having one as long as possible. However, after being at a level-4 dilation for several hours and learning that Rylen's oxygen level was dropping, Brittney and Allan took the doctor's advice and opted for a C-section.

Allan sat nervously in a waiting room, praying, waiting to be summoned by a nurse into Brittney's operating room. There he sat—wearing his goofy hospital-issued blue smock and muffin cap, hoping the nurse wouldn't forget him. But at the perfect moment, Allan was wheeled into the OR, and he was at Brittney's side as Rylen let out his very first cry. After the nurses ensured Rylen was healthy and breathing normally, Allan was handed the scissors and given the privilege of cutting the umbilical cord. As Allan gazed in shocked disbelief at his newborn son, he wanted nothing more than to hold him in his arms. He was instantly smitten ... instantly in love.

On May 26, 2016, Allan and Brittney's first miracle baby was born. And on this occasion, both their hopes and dreams were realized. Both mom and son were perfectly healthy. Allan felt he was the most blessed man on the planet. He was married to the most beautiful woman—inside and out. And he was holding in his arms the most handsome baby boy he'd ever laid eyes on. Just forty-eight hours later, both Brittney and Rylen were ready to join Allan on the short journey back home.

After her C-section, Brittney wasn't able to drive for the next eight weeks. Since Allan couldn't drive either, their parents pitched in to help with errands and doctors' visits. But despite his physical limitations, Allan was Superdad at home. He helped with changings, feedings, burpings and nap time. He knew that Brittney needed time to heal, so he did everything he could to lighten her load and let both her and Rylen know they were deeply loved.

Allan and Brittney had learned the truth of Romans 8:28: "And we know that in all things God works for the good of those who love Him, who are called according to His purpose." With God there is always a silver lining running through every problem, trial or illness we face. And the silver lining running through Allan's arachnoiditis was crystal clear during Rylen's first year of life.

While there were many things that Allan *wasn't* able to do with his son—give him a bath, toss him in the air or give him a traditional piggyback ride—Allan was able to give Rylen a precious gift that most dads *can't* give their sons ... his time. Lots and lots of undistracted time. Since Allan wasn't able to work outside the home, he devoted himself full-time to his precious wife and son. And he wouldn't have traded it for the world.

Never being one to let his physical limitations sideline him, Allan found ways to improvise as a wheelchair-bound father. Although he couldn't give Rylen a bath, he could join Brittney and Rylen in the bathroom and make bath time more fun than a barrel of monkeys. Even though Rylen couldn't soar like Superman over Allan's head, he could soar like Superman in Allan's lap. And nothing could top the one-of-a-kind, pedal-to-the-metal piggyback rides that his daddy gave him. How cool it was to stand on the back of his daddy's powerchair with his arms draped around his hero's neck as Allan pushed the joystick forward at full throttle.

Both Allan and Brittney loved being parents. Little Rylen made their family more complete. But they quietly wondered if God might, in His perfect timing, bless them with a second miracle. Allan had his Mini-Me. It would be nice if Brittney had a little girl to follow in her footsteps. And on January 30, 2019, Allan and Brittney took another trip over the moon.

On that day, Brittney took a pregnancy test, and the two little pink lines shouted loud and clear, "Baby #2 is on his/her way!"

Right away Brittney scheduled an appointment with her OB-GYN, but during her visit, a nurse gave her disappointing news. She said Brittney wasn't pregnant, but she ordered bloodwork just to make sure. Unfortunately, the results wouldn't be in until after the weekend. Although he was worried and scared, Allan turned to the nurse and told her, "It's going to be okay. There's a baby. It's just too early to hear the heartbeat." The next 72 hours were slower than a snail on the Sabbath, but the sound of their second baby's heartbeat on Monday made it worth the wait.

A few weeks later, on Superbowl Sunday, Allan and Brittney shared the good news with their family. When they did, the "Big Game" seemed like old news. The New England Patriots versus the Los Angeles Rams—who really cared? The Schwartz family had something much more exciting to celebrate.

Over the next several months, it was déjà vu: Cautious optimism. Nervous anticipation. Ultrasound. Follow-up ultrasound. Heartbeat. Growing tummy. Kicks. And the big question: "Should we find out whether we're having a boy or a girl?" That was easy to answer: *Absolutely*!

About halfway through Brittney's pregnancy, Allan and Brittney were told the great news, "It's a girl!" A boy for him and a girl for her—it was a dream come true, especially after wondering for years if the doctors were right when they predicted that Allan would never become a father. Now, if all went smoothly during the final months of Brittney's pregnancy, Allan would be a father two times over.

After discussing a few names, Allan and Brittney settled on the name Tenley Ann. And, just as they had with Rylen, they gave her a middle name in honor of one of their loved family members: Allan's Nana Ann. On September 23, 2019, Brittney and Allan returned to St. Mary Medical Center with Brittney's overnight bag in hand. Since it was a scheduled C-section, this delivery was smoother than Rylen's. As Allan held his precious little girl in his arms for the first time, he was smitten once again.

She was every bit as perfect as newborn Rylen had been—fearfully and wonderfully crafted by God. But at the same time, she seemed so different. She was a new creation, perfectly unique and beautiful in her own way. She was quiet and sweet, but early in life she showed signs of being independent and feisty. Without a doubt, Mom and Dad would have to keep a close eye on her. But through it all, they knew that she'd bring their family of four a whole lot of joy and laughter. She was hand-picked by God to be their daughter—their sweet little princess.

On a cool winter evening as Allan reclined in his favorite chair with Tenley in his arms and Rylen asleep beside him, he felt like the richest man on earth. He was in his happy spot. He had a beautiful wife who loved him, a son who adored him and a gorgeous baby girl who felt safe and content in her daddy's arms. His quiver was full, and he knew he couldn't keep the blessing to himself. God had shown him a taste of the goodness that awaits one of Christ's followers on the other side of pain and suffering. Allan was not only *seeing* but *experiencing* the light at the end of the tunnel. His perseverance had paid off. And He knew God had chosen him to share this simple, life-changing message with the world.

CHAPTER 18

THE PERSEVERANCE CONFERENCE

*"And let us consider how we may spur one
another on toward love and good deeds."*
- Hebrews 10:24

Allan has never been one to let the grass grow under the wheels of his powerchair. Within minutes of becoming the youngest person at Johns Hopkins to be diagnosed with arachnoiditis, he began to embrace his calling. With all his heart he believed God had a purpose for his disease. He didn't think God had *caused* it, but He believed God had a plan to *use* it. And as the days passed, it became more and more clear to Allan that God's plan involved him sharing his story with others. One way or another, he felt called to be a motivational speaker—inspiring people to place their trust in Jesus Christ and to persevere through their unique trials and tribulations.

Just a few months after returning home from Johns Hopkins, Allan was given the opportunity to share his testimony in Upland, California, at the home church of one of his former teachers from Western High School. Over the course of several weeks, Allan spent many hours reflecting on his journey, searching the Scriptures and putting his story down on paper. At points his notes resembled chicken scratch more than a life-changing message of inspiration and hope. But when he rolled up to the front of the sanctuary and started speaking, Allan's message came alive.

The Sunday morning crowd topped one hundred adults and teens. Allan spoke for about thirty minutes to a very attentive audience. As Allan walked them though his painful and faith-stretching journey over the past three years, some of the men and women in the crowd looked visibly shaken—as if Allan were sharing the details of being tortured and left to die.

Although Allan didn't shy away from sharing some of the details of his painful journey, his main focus was on the fact that it was nothing short of a miracle that he was still alive. That being the case, Allan emphasized his determination to persevere and never give up. And he encouraged his listeners to do the same: persevere and never give up. In the minutes that followed his message, over a dozen people came to the front of the room asking for prayer.

Near the end of the service, the pastor asked for permission to lay hands on Allan and pray for him. Of course, Allan eagerly agreed. Over the next few minutes, the room erupted with cries to God for a miracle—a complete transformation of Allan's health. They prayed in faith, *believing* that Allan was about to get his miracle. In faith, Allan believed it too. And God *did* answer their prayers of faith. Just not in the way they had imagined. In the months that followed, God made it abundantly clear that His answer was *No* ... at least for now. He was *not* going to heal Allan of arachnoiditis until He had finished using it for His glory.

As the months passed, other speaking opportunities began to trickle in. More times than not, Allan was asked to speak at a church. But on several occasions, he was asked to speak at a Christian high school and share with the students—who weren't much younger than him—how important it is to *not* take life for granted but to seize the moment to be strong and courageous for Jesus Christ. Just as Brittney had found it difficult to wrap her mind around the fact that such a young man was confined to a wheelchair, many of the high school students struggled to do the same. But he got them thinking, *really* thinking, about how fragile life is and what matters most.

Although Allan attended a six-week Introduction to Preaching class at his home church, that was the extent of his formal training for public speaking. No college classes. No seminary. No seminars titled "Motivational Speaking 101." Allan just kept saying "Yes!" to speaking opportunities and leaning on God as he prepared and delivered his messages. And because he had a network of several thousand friends on social media, speaking engagements came quite often. In the fourteen years since speaking at his high school teacher's church, Allan has accepted dozens of speaking engagements.

Whether he was speaking at a church, a school or a conference, Allan savored every opportunity God gave Him to deliver a clear message of hope and encouragement. But at the same time, Allan felt led to create and host a conference of his own—one that would both lead unbelievers to Jesus Christ *and* inspire Christians to persevere through their trials. He bounced the idea off Brittney, his parents and his pastor. After receiving a strong thumbs up from all of them, he started making plans for his first inspirational conference in 2014.

As Allan reached out to several pastors, worship leaders and motivational speakers, his vision for the conference was dialed in. He envisioned an event that lasted just a few hours on a Saturday and included at least three great worship music leaders, several inspiring Christian speakers (including himself) and some good food. Simple enough, right?

Not so much.

It's a good thing that Allan has thick skin and doesn't get bent out of shape when told "No!" Allan quickly discovered that getting pastors, speakers and worship musicians to leave the four walls of their own church buildings to do ministry together elsewhere is no small feat. While many of them applauded Allan for his God-honoring vision and offered their prayers and encouragement, most weren't ready to commit to attending the conference or inviting their church families to give it a try.

In their defense, pastors and church leaders are responsible before God to make sure their church members are being taught God's word faithfully. And most of those Allan reached out to didn't know him very well. Was Allan's teaching sound? Was the conference just a dream, or would it really happen? Was any church sponsoring him, or was he somehow going rogue?

All valid questions, but they didn't help Allan get the job done. So, as a result, his first attempt at putting together an inspirational conference failed. The event didn't happen. So, Allan rolled up his ministry sleeves and tried again the next year. Same result. But for Allan, the third time was the charm. In June 2016, Allan hosted his first one-day conference in a small, 30' x 30' room on the campus of his alma mater: Apple Valley Christian School. Allan called it The Ignite Conference, and on the day of the event, around seventy-five people (mostly family and friends) showed up and packed into the small room to see what Allan had put together.

From the look of things, everyone's expectations were surpassed. As Allan's friends walked into the school building on the day of the conference, they were immediately impressed. In the entryway, Allan's wife and sister had the registration table running like clockwork. The conference room was set up, music was playing, and the crowd had already started to gather. And when the live worship music began, I was just one of the many attenders who had the same gut feeling: "This is 'legit!' This is really, REALLY good!" There was no doubt that the Spirit of Christ was in the room, and He was *definitely* working through the energetic, Jesus-loving young man on wheels.

Each of the three worship leaders was talented and radiated God's love. And during the conference, the two keynote speakers, Allan and myself, spoke about the goodness and faithfulness of God. To be honest, I was shocked that the event even happened. I had agreed to speak at each of Allan's conferences that had failed to materialize for two years running. So, if I'd been a betting man, I would have wagered that this one wouldn't happen either. That'll teach me to bet against Allan! His whole life over the past ten years had been about defying the odds.

The highlight of the conference was when Allan rolled up front and shared his testimony—his story of learning to overcome the challenges of living with this strange bedfellow called arachnoiditis. Many of the attenders had never heard even half of Allan's story, and they were blown away by what they heard. Hearing of Allan's multiple doctors' visits, epidurals, spinal taps, misdiagnoses and surgeries was eye-opening. Learning of Allan's perpetual level-10 pain caused them to grimace in pain themselves. And hearing how many times Allan's hopes and dreams were shattered caused their hearts to drop.

But once again, Allan's trials, pain and unanswered prayers weren't the point of his message. God's grace and mercy were. Allan so beautifully described how, in His mercy, God had given him the strength to deal with more pain than he ever thought possible. In His *grace*, God had given him opportunities to speak hope into hurting people's lives, encouraging them to persevere through their own difficulties. In His *mercy*, God had held his disease at bay, keeping it from traveling to his brain and snuffing out his life. And in His *love*, God had given him multiple opportunities to share the life-saving message of Jesus Christ with unbelievers, leading many of them to salvation. Allan believed with all his heart, *If one life is changed through my story, if one person begins to feel there is a reason to live, then it is worth all the hell I've been through.*

As the Ignite Conference came to a close, there was a consensus in the room: "Allan, you've GOT to do this again next year! But you'd better find a bigger room, because people *need* this. They *really* need this!"

Allan was ecstatic. His family and friends were catching the fire. Now they not only admired and supported his vision, they could see what he had seen in his mind's eye. And just a few months later, in October 2016, the Perseverance Conference was born. Allan created it as an annual one-day event that would encourage and uplift people through music and inspirational messages that would lead them closer to Christ.

In the months that followed, Allan kicked into overdrive and made all the necessary preparations for his First Annual Perseverance Conference. When the day came, over two hundred people packed into a much larger room at a conference center in Ontario, California. Most were first-timers. And once again, Allan and his hand-picked, prayed-over team of worship leaders and speakers didn't disappoint. With a deep sense of spiritual hunger, people cried out to God in worship. Many came forward for prayer, and several made first-time decisions to become believers and followers of Jesus Christ. It was remarkable!

And it continues to be remarkable. Even during the Covid-19 pandemic of 2020 and 2021, Allan persevered with his Perseverance Conference. In 2020, it was completely online, but it was still a powerful, inspirational conference for the several hundred who attended. Some years the attendance has been higher than others. But regardless of the turnout, there has always been an impact. Pain is embraced. Relationships are healed. Hope is restored. And Jesus Christ is glorified.

The Perseverance Conference is just one of the many ministries of encouragement and hope that Allan oversees. He continues to make himself available as a guest speaker at churches in and around Southern California. He serves as an Elder at his home church: Impact Christian Church in Victorville. And in his new weekly podcast, he tackles tough questions people are asking about God and the Bible. In typical Allan fashion, he shoots straight but does so with a big dose of Christ-centered hope, encouragement and joy.

The young man in the powerchair continues to inspire many toward love, good deeds and perseverance. His influence is significant, because anyone who knows him knows: He's the real deal. Allan doesn't just talk the talk; he walks the walk ... even on wheels. He doesn't just *believe* in drawing closer to God; he actually *does* it. He doesn't just *believe* in miracles; he *is* a miracle. And he doesn't just *believe* God called him to persevere. He actually *perseveres!* And at the age of 34, he shows no signs of letting up.

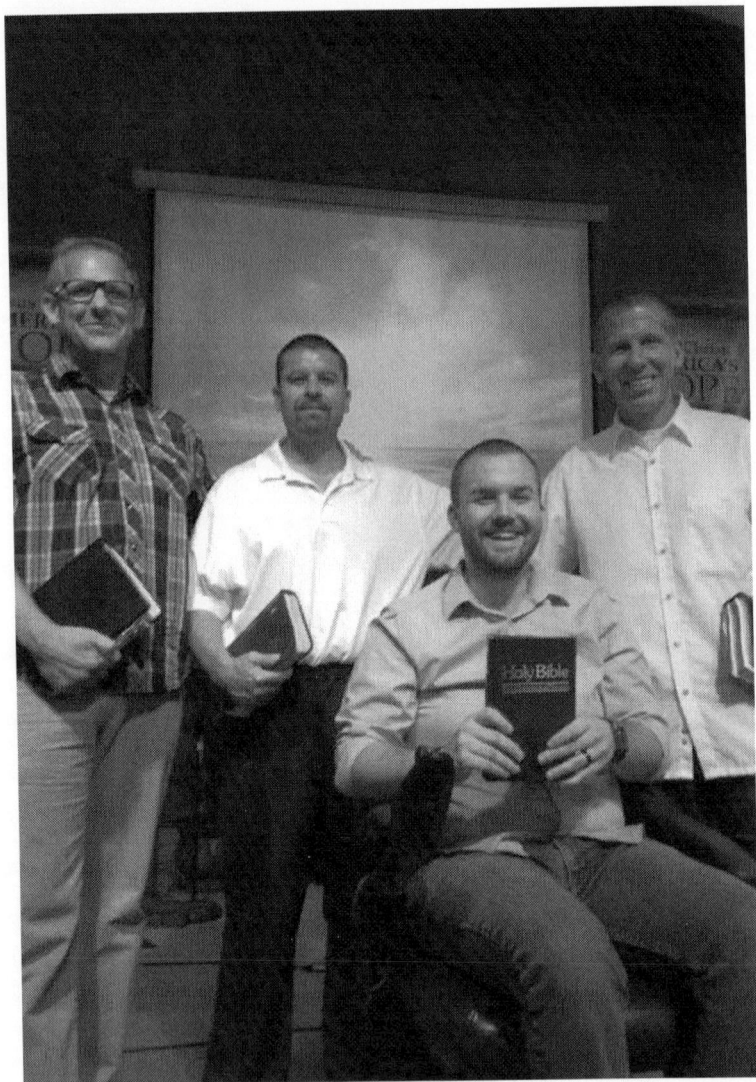

After preaching one of his first Sunday morning sermons, Allan poses with Pastor Dane and two friends from First Christian Church's Preaching Class.

PART FIVE

10 DAYS TO PERSEVERE

A 10-DAY DEVOTIONAL

An Introduction to 10 Days to Persevere

"These commandments that I give you today are to be upon your hearts. Impress them on your children. Talk about them when you sit at home and when you walk along the road, when you lie down and when you get up."
- Deuteronomy 6:6-7

Early in the process of writing Allan's biography, I knew I wanted to share with you some of his favorite Bible verses—Scriptures that have inspired him and given him the wisdom and strength to persevere. Although there are dozens of verses from both the Old and New Testaments that he loves and has drawn hope from during his journey, I asked Allan to narrow his list down to ten. I'm grateful to have this opportunity to share these verses with you in the form of a 10-day devotional.

10 Days to Persevere was written with you in mind. Allan and I both want you to draw strength and hope from his favorite Bible verses. They have helped Allan persevere through his trials, and we believe they will help you persevere through your trials as well. Over the years, Allan has come back to these verses again and again as he's battled pain, fear and disappointment with God. And we hope and pray you'll do the same.

To get the most out of these next ten chapters, you will need to pace yourself. God's word can't be handled like a junior high life science study guide. Scripture can't be crammed. Allan wasn't transformed by these Bible verses overnight and you won't be either. Allan is a work in progress, and so are you. The word of God needs time to soak deeply into your mind and heart. It is living, active and is more patient than you are. So, don't rush the reading of these next ten chapters. Sure, because they're short, you could read all ten of them one after the other in under an hour. But if you do, you'll be selling yourself short. You'll be missing out on some of the blessings God will only give if you take the time necessary to hide His word in your heart.

So, I encourage you to restrain your inner Speedy Gonzales and read one devotional per day over the next ten days. You'll need to carve out at least fifteen minutes each day to do your devotional at a time and place where you can pay attention and be free of distractions. And, realizing that daily devotionals are a new thing for many Christians, I've made this guide easy to follow. Here's how to do it in five easy steps:

PRAY. Ask God to open your ears and speak to you through His Word.

READ. Carefully read the Bible verse and the commentary that follows.

MEDITATE. Think about what you've just read.

PRAY. Pray the sample prayer included at the end of each chapter.

WRITE. Jot down some thoughts, reflections or action points in the space provided.

If Christian meditation is new to you, don't worry. You

already know how to do it. Years ago, I heard a pastor say, "If you know how to worry, you know how to meditate." To worry is to fix your thoughts on something *negative*. To meditate is to fix your thoughts on something *positive*. That make sense, doesn't it? You're already an expert at thinking about the depressing things of this world that weigh you down. Over the next ten days, you have a chance to get better at thinking about the inspiring things of God that will lift you up. God has used these ten Bible verses to do an extraordinary work in Allan's life, and I believe they could do an extraordinary work in your life as well.

So, are you ready for our 10-day journey together? If so, pray this prayer with me; then turn the page for Day 1.

Pray with me...

Father in heaven, You are amazing! Thank You for being my Creator and my God. Thank You for sending Jesus Christ to die on the cross for my sins so that I could enjoy a relationship with You. Father, I want to learn more about You and learn from Your Word how to persevere through my trials. So, I give this next 10 days to You. Show me Your strength. Teach me Your ways. And help me to trust, love and obey You better than ever. In Jesus' name, Amen.

DAY 1: COME TO ME

*"Come to Me, all you who are weary and
burdened, and I will give you rest."*
- Matthew 11:28

Jesus invites you to come. How will you respond?

The Message paraphrases Jesus' words in Matthew 11:28 this way:
*"Are you tired? Worn out? Burned out on religion? Come to me. Get
away with Me and you'll recover your life. I'll show you how to take
a real rest."* Take a moment to ponder each question and answer it
honestly:

Are you tired?

Are you worn out?

Are you burned out on religion?

Chances are, you answered at least one of these questions with a
"Yes." Many of us travel through life at breakneck speed. We're
always on the go. Our schedules are jam-packed. And we don't

give our bodies or minds enough time to rest and recharge. Since God created our bodies, minds and spirits to be interconnected, this feverish pace takes a toll on our relationship with God.

Allan was taught this hard lesson as a young man battling his mystery disease. As he rushed from doctor to doctor, hospital to hospital and clinic to clinic, he found himself tired, worn out and feeling distant from God. It felt as if he and his family had the weight of the world on their shoulders, and Allan didn't think he could handle another doctor's visit, round of lab work or misdiagnosis. His burden was too heavy, and he needed help shouldering it.

And Jesus Christ did just that. He didn't completely *remove* Allan's burden, but He stepped in to help Allan *shoulder* it. In fact, Jesus switched backpacks with Allan. Jesus gave Allan his light pack, and He Himself took the heavy one. He began working tirelessly on Allan's behalf, and He reassured him that He would be with him. Jesus gave Allan the strength he needed to keep him from wearing out. In short, He gave Allan rest for his soul.

Jesus Christ can do the same for you. He is ready and willing to switch packs with you—taking the heavy burden off your shoulders and replacing it with His lighter one. He is ready to work tirelessly on your behalf. (He already proved that on the cross.) He has the strength you need to keep from wearing out. He can reignite your flame of passion for God that may have begun to flicker. And He would love to give you rest for your soul.

Jesus invites you to come. So, how will you respond?

PRAY WITH ME...

Lord Jesus, thank You for Your invitation to come. Lately I've been feeling a bit tired, drained and burned out. I've been running around like crazy trying to carry my burdens on my own. Please forgive me and help me. I need Your comfort, peace and rest for my soul. Thank You for offering me Your light burden and carrying the heavier one for me. Please remind me throughout the day to come to you with my *hardest* questions, my *biggest* problems and my *heaviest* burdens. And help me to rest in the comfort of knowing You will help me deal with each of them masterfully in Your perfect timing. In Jesus' name, Amen.

NOTES:
thoughts, reflections & action points

Day 2: I Stand at the Door and Knock

"Here I am! I stand at the door and knock.
If anyone hears My voice and opens the door,
I will come in and eat with him, and he with Me."
- Revelation 3:20

Sadly, many Christians leave Jesus out in the cold.

Although Christians today normally only quote Revelation 3:20 while urging unbelievers to open their hearts to Christ, Jesus actually spoke these words to Christians in the Laodicean church. A few verses earlier, Jesus told them, "I know you deeds, that you are neither cold nor hot. I wish you were either one or the other! So, because you are lukewarm—neither hot nor cold—I am about to spit you out of My mouth."

Harsh words? Absolutely! But as Jesus explains in verse 19: "Those whom I love I rebuke and discipline. So be earnest, and repent." So, think about, REALLY think about, what Jesus is saying to Christians ... what He is saying to you: *Half-hearted Christianity—Christianity where you just go through the motions and pretend to make*

Me a priority—makes Me sick to My stomach. It makes Me want to puke. I love you too much to keep quiet. So, I'm rebuking you, disciplining you and patiently knocking at your heart's door ... urging you to repent and invite Me into the center of your life once again.

So, do Christians ever shut out Jesus? Sadly, yes. In fact, Christians do it all the time. There were times in Allan's life when he put Jesus on the back burner. Sports were all-consuming. Doing his coach's will was a higher priority than doing the Lord's will. Time with friends was more important than time with God. Work was a higher priority than worship. When you think about it, idolatry is easier than you think ... even for Christians. At its most basic level, idolatry is the act of prioritizing *anyone* or *anything* higher than Jesus. And it's very easy to invite any number of people and things into the center of our lives while subtly pushing Jesus out the door. So, ask yourself...

Have I been prioritizing anyone or anything higher than Jesus?

Have I been subtly pushing Jesus out the door?

Is Jesus knocking at my heart's door—asking me to let Him back in?

Do I need to repent (make a spiritual U-turn) and invite Jesus back into the center of my life?

If you answered "Yes!" to any of these questions and find your answer unsettling, I suggest you spend a few minutes in humble prayer. We all need to spend some time opening our hearts' doors wide to Jesus Christ. There are two suggested prayers below. If you are a baptized believer and follower of Jesus Christ who has, in one way or another, pushed Jesus out of the driver's seat of your life, I encourage you to pray the first prayer: *A Prayer for Christians.*

And for those of you who want to become a Christian—to make a first-time decision to trust and obey Jesus Christ as your Savior and Lord—I encourage you to pray the second prayer: *A Prayer to Become a Follower of Jesus.* Today is the day to have your sins forgiven. Today is the day to begin a life-changing relationship with God. Today is the day to reserve your spot in heaven. Today is the day to become a believer and follower of Jesus Christ.

A PRAYER FOR CHRISTIANS

Heavenly Father, I come to You in Jesus' name asking for Your mercy and forgiveness. I believe with all my heart that Jesus Christ is King of Kings and Lord of Lords, but You'd never know it by the way I've been treating You recently. I have prioritized people and things above Jesus. I have put my Lord on the back burner, and, without even realizing it, I've pushed Him out the door. I admit my sin, and I'm ready to repent and turn from my sin. If You need to rebuke and discipline me, I will receive it ... whatever it takes to get right with my Lord Jesus once again. Lord Jesus, I open the door of my life to You right now. Please come in and take the driver's seat once again. You are my highest priority, my first love and my greatest joy. In Jesus' name, Amen.

A PRAYER TO BECOME A FOLLOWER OF JESUS

Heavenly Father, at times I've thought I was *good enough* on my own and didn't need You. But I was wrong. I need Jesus. I

ADMIT that I am a sinner, and I need Jesus to be my Savior. I BELIEVE Jesus is the Son of God who came to earth and died on the cross for my sins. And I CHOOSE today to open the door of my heart to You, Jesus, and place You in the driver's seat of my life. I am ready to trust You, love You and obey Your commands from this day forward. Today I'm becoming a follower of Jesus Christ. Thank You, Lord, for saving me. In Jesus' name, Amen.

NOTES:
thoughts, reflections & action points

DAY 3: I NEED YOU TO GO

*"He told them, 'The harvest is plentiful, but the workers
are few. Ask the Lord of the harvest, therefore,
to send out workers into His harvest field.'"*
- Luke 10:2

In a hospital bed 2,500 miles from home, he said *Yes!* to God's
call.

Within minutes of receiving his diagnosis of arachnoiditis, Allan
said *Yes!* to God's call to become a motivational speaker, sharing
Christ's message of hope and grace with discouraged and hurting
people. God inspired Allan to be a perseverance poster boy,
modeling for others how to trust and follow our great and
awesome God in the eye of the storm. Allan said *Yes!* to God's call,
and so should you.

You see, the harvest of human souls is plentiful, but the workers
are few. Consider how Jesus' inspiring words are translated in a
few other English versions:

"A large crop is in the fields, but there are only a few workers. Ask the Lord in charge of the harvest to send out
workers to bring it in."
(Contemporary English Version)

"Plead with the Lord of the harvest to send out more
laborers to help you, for the harvest is so plentiful and the
workers so few.
(The Living Bible)

"There are a great many people to harvest. But there are
only a few workers to harvest them. God owns the
harvest. Pray to God that He will send more workers to
help gather His harvest.
(International Children's Bible)

Bottom line: All around you there are men and women, boys and
girls, who need Jesus. Your parents, your siblings, your kids, your
neighbors, your coworkers, your neighbors, even the annoying
lady in the line in front of you at Walmart. *Everyone* needs Jesus.
The harvest is plentiful. The problem is ... the workers are few.
There are far more "Christians" than "workers," because far too
many Christians refuse to do Christ's most *important* work.

But Allan refused to be a Christian who plugged his ears to the
call of God. In his hospital room in Baltimore, Maryland, Allan
said, *Here I am. Send me.* Despite being the youngest man in the
nation diagnosed with his incurable neurological disease, Allan
said, *Yes!* to God. Despite his recurring level-10 pain, Allan said,
Yes! to God. And despite the fact that he would most likely spend
the rest of his life in a wheelchair and could die in a matter of
minutes if the arachnoiditis spread to his brain, Allan still said,
Yes! to God.

If anyone had reasonable excuses for saying *No!* to God, Allan did.

But Allan said *Yes!* anyway. And so should you, because the stakes are so high. People are *living* every day without hope and purpose. Others are *dying* every day without salvation and peace with God. In the harvest field of your community, precious lives hang in the balance. And our Lord Jesus is counting on you and me to say *Yes!* to His call to be His workers in the harvest field.

God won't likely call you to be a motivational speaker like Allan. But if you have just recently made a decision to become a follower of Jesus, He is calling you to be publicly baptized in water. You need to do that as soon as possible, proclaiming to people around you that Jesus has changed your life for the better, and He can change their lives too.

He is also calling you to share Christ's hope and grace in the part of God's harvest field that is closest to you: your own home. God has strategically placed you in your family to shine Christ's light, pray for your family members and lead them to Christ. God is also calling you to become an active part of a good Bible-teaching church that reaches beyond the four walls of the building to share Christ's hope and grace with your community. Finally, somehow, someway, God is calling you to "go." More than anything else, your community needs Jesus Christ. So, more than anything else, your community needs Christ's message of hope and grace that you have to share.

PRAY WITH ME...

Heavenly Father, I am a *Christian*, but I haven't been a very consistent *worker*. I want that to change today. You loved the world so much that You gave Your one and only Son to die on the cross for our sins. People around me need to hear that life-changing message, to have the chance to be forgiven and to have a relationship with God. So, Holy Spirit, give me the wisdom to speak the *right* words at the *right* time, and give me boldness to speak when You lead me to speak. When You need work to be done, help me to always be ready and willing to say, *Here I am. Send me.* In Jesus' name, Amen.

NOTES:
thoughts, reflections & action points

Day 4: My Plans Are Better

"'For I know the plans I have for you,' declares
the LORD, 'plans to prosper you and not to harm
you, plans to give you hope and a future.'"
- Jeremiah 29:11

God's plans are better than your plans ... MUCH better.

Never in a million years would Allan have planned to have a debilitating spinal cord disease. He never would have orchestrated plans to have back surgery at the age of 17 or to be in a wheelchair at the age of 18. He never would have planned to experience level-10 pain every day, to be dependent upon caregivers or to put his parents through a financial nightmare. He had no desire to give up his dreams of being a professional athlete or of walking down the aisle with his beautiful bride on his wedding day.

In the early years of Allan's disease, he felt devastated as his plans were wrecked and his dreams didn't come to pass. None of it made sense. He loved God. He had given his life to Jesus Christ. He had been a "good" kid who was on his way to becoming a respectable adult. Then God unexpectedly threw a wrench in Allan's works, turning his whole world upside down.

But God tells us in Isaiah 55:8-9: "'For My thoughts are not your thoughts, neither are your ways My ways,' declares the LORD. 'As the heavens are higher than the earth, so are My ways higher than your ways and My thoughts than your thoughts.'"

Allan had to come to grips with the reality that God's thoughts, ways and plans have to be embraced *by faith*, because in the moments when Allan's whole body was hollering in pain, God's *thoughts* didn't make sense. His *ways* felt harsh and cruel. And His *plans* seemed ludicrous. Allan found himself crying out in prayer, *"God, what are doing? None of this makes any sense!"*

Can you relate? Is it safe to say that if you had had your way, you wouldn't have gone through half the junk you've gone through in life: the physical injuries, the broken relationships, loved ones passing, dashed hopes and shattered dreams? Throughout your lifetime you've experienced your fair share of pain and suffering, and, honestly, it's only just begun. There's more to come.

That's why it's critical that you settle this reality in your mind and heart once and for all: GOD IS GOOD, HE KNOWS WHAT HE'S DOING, AND HE IS WORTHY OF YOUR TRUST. Despite what your five senses are telling you, believe that God is good. Even when you don't understand what God is doing, be confident that *He* knows what He's doing. And even when you are surrounded by people who are suspicious of God's motives, trust in Him with all your heart.

He is all-knowing. He is all-powerful. And He loves you more than anyone else in the universe could *ever* love you. So, no matter what pain and suffering life brings you, believe God when He tells you, "I know the plans I have for you, plans to prosper you and not to harm you, plans to give you hope and a future."

PRAY WITH ME...

Heavenly Father, I praise you for being all-knowing, all-powerful and good all the time. Your thoughts are *higher* than my thoughts; Your ways are *higher* than my ways, and Your plans are so much *better* than my plans. So, I believe You when You tell me You have good plans for my life, plans to prosper me and not to harm me, plans to give me hope and a future. *Your* plans for me are so much better than *my* plans for me. So, help me to trust You today—walking by faith and not by sight. Help me to trust completely in Your goodness, wisdom and strength so that I may walk in step with Your good plans for me. In Jesus' name, Amen.

NOTES:
thoughts, reflections & action points

Day 5: Joy Awaits in Strange Places

"Consider it pure joy, my brothers, whenever you face trials of many kinds, because you know that the testing of your faith develops perseverance. Perseverance must finish its work so that you may be mature and complete, not lacking anything."
- James 1:2-4

How would you describe *pure joy* in five words or less?

Here are a few possibilities to get your gears turning:

Holding a newborn baby
A wedding day kiss
A sunset in paradise
A perfectly cooked steak
Being pampered at the spa
A peaceful morning fishing
Meeting your favorite celebrity

Now, take a few moments to fill in the blank: To me, pure joy is

_____

_____.

But notice how James fills in the blank. Pure joy is "facing trials of many kinds" (James 1:2). That's rather odd and unexpected, isn't it? Who actually thinks that way?

Woohoo! I just received an eviction notice.

Let's celebrate! I just got fired from my job.

It's party time! My doctor just told me I have cancer.

I've never been happier! My best friend just told me to "Get lost!"

Again I ask: *Who actually thinks that way?* According to James, mature Christians do ... or at least they *should*. And Allan is living proof that it *can* be done. His face radiates joy because he has long embraced this biblical truth: God NEVER wastes pain; In God's kingdom, pain ALWAYS has a purpose. So, even when Allan doesn't understand *why* God allows his pain and suffering to linger, he tries to remember to smile and thank God anyway.

In 1 Thessalonians 5:18, God's word tells us to "give thanks in all circumstances, for this is God's will for you in Christ Jesus." I bet you'd agree: It's hard to give thanks *in* all circumstances; it's even harder to give thanks *for* all circumstances. But, believe it or not, by God's grace Allan not only thanks God *in spite* of his pain and suffering, at times he is able to thank God *for* his pain and suffering. At times God gives him the strength to say, *Thank You, Lord, for my arachnoiditis.*

You see, arachnoiditis, just like every other trial God allows to come our way, has a silver lining. Allan's life-threatening disease has helped him develop an extraordinary measure of stamina, which has led him down an enviable path of becoming "mature and complete, not lacking anything." Most people look at Allan and focus on what he *can't* do: walk down the street, ride a bike, drive a car or do a single jumping jack. But they miss what Allan *can* do much better than most: savor the small blessings in life, successfully navigate unexpected obstacles and squeeze every bit of joy out of every day he lives.

Turns out, joy is at our fingertips every day—even in the middle of our trials. In fact, for those of us who follow Christ, trials are the *key* to unlocking the joy in the seemingly tedious, painful or mundane moments in our lives. So, take a lesson from Allan. When trials come your way ... count it all joy.

PRAY WITH ME...

Heavenly Father, I'm not very good at thanking You *in* my trials. I'm even worse at thanking You *for* my trials. But I'd like to change that today. With Your help, I *will* change. Help me to never forget that because You are Love, no trial can ever come my way that hasn't first passed through the filter of Your love for me. Please teach me to count it all joy: for better, for worse, for richer, for poorer, in sickness and in health. Even when I'm going through a trial that includes pain, hardship or disappointment, I want to rejoice. Because of Your love and grace, I know my pain *always* has a purpose, and You won't waste *any* of it. Thank You, Father. I love You, and I trust You. In Jesus' name, Amen.

NOTES:
thoughts, reflections & action points

Day 6: There's No Comparison

"I consider that our present sufferings are not worth comparing with the glory that will be revealed in us."
- Romans 8:18

No pain, no gain.

Take a look with me at how Romans 8:18 is translated in several other English translations.

> "Yet what we suffer now is nothing compared to the glory He will give us later."
> (The Living Bible)

> "I consider our present sufferings insignificant compared to the glory that will soon be revealed to us."
> (God's Word Translation)

> "I don't think there's any comparison between the present hard times and the coming good times."
> (The Message)

Olympic athletes, cancer patients, mothers of newborns, and POWs can all attest to this fact: Human beings are capable of enduring intense pain over long periods of time ... *if* there is a light at the end of the tunnel. *If* there is an Olympic medal in reach. *If* there is the hope of a cure. *If* the baby in the birth canal will soon be in your arms. *If* you know your platoon is coming back to rescue you.

In Romans 8:17, the Apostle Paul shares an important insight that many Christians would rather ignore: *If we are going to share Jesus' future glory in heaven, we must first share His present sufferings on earth.* Not very enticing, is it? Especially when we consider that Jesus was "despised and rejected by men, a man of sorrows, and familiar with suffering" (Isaiah 53:3). But Jesus makes it clear in the New Testament that if He (our Lord) had sorrows, we *too* will have sorrows. If He was rejected, we *too* will be rejected. And if He had to endure pain and suffering, we *too* will have to endure pain and suffering.

So that begs the question: *Is all the sorrow, rejection, pain and suffering worth it in the long run? Is there a bright enough light at the end of the tunnel to justify enduring it?* And in Romans 8:18, God answers these questions with a resounding *Yes!* What we suffer now "is nothing compared to the glory He will give us later." Our present sufferings are "insignificant compared to the glory that will soon be revealed to us." There's really "[no] comparison between the present hard times and the coming good times."

As Allan has come to accept (for the most part) his pain and immobility, He has come to believe *not only* that God doesn't waste pain and that all pain has a purpose here on earth. He has also come to believe that all his pain and suffering is achieving for him an immeasurable weight of glory in eternity. Every ounce of his pain here on earth will result in a hundred pounds of blessing in heaven. Every doctor's visit. Every poke of the needle. Every failed treatment. Every misdiagnosis. Every second in his wheel-chair and every moment of level-10 pain. ALL of it is infinitely *meaningful*, because God will see to it that not an ounce of it goes to waste. Every bit of it will pay off in the long run. God is using every moment of Allan's pain and suffering for His glory ... and, in time, for Allan's glory.

The same holds true for you. Every ounce of your pain and suffering here on earth will result in a hundred pounds of glory in heaven ... *if* that pain and suffering was endured for Christ and His kingdom work. If your pain and suffering are the result of your own sin and selfishness, you can't expect an eternal reward. But if your pain and suffering have come your way as you've walked the narrow road of trusting, loving and obeying Jesus Christ's commands, your immeasurable reward awaits you. "As it is written: 'No eye has seen, no ear has heard, no mind has conceived what God has prepared for those who love Him.'" (1 Corinthians 2:9).

PRAY WITH ME...

Heavenly Father, please forgive me for being short-sighted. Sometimes I can't see the forest for the trees. I get so caught up in the pain, suffering and disappointment in my life here on earth that I lose sight of the far-surpassing glory that awaits me in heaven. I forget that my temporary troubles will one day seem insignificant compared to my eternal rewards. So, help me fix my eyes on the prize and walk obediently down your narrow path that leads to eternal life. Help me to see the light at the end of the tunnel. Help me to believe with all my heart that everything, ABSOLUTELY EVERYTHING, I endure for Christ here on earth will be richly rewarded in heaven. In Jesus' name, Amen.

NOTES:
thoughts, reflections & action points

DAY 7: I AM AT WORK FOR YOUR GOOD

"And we know that in all things God works
for the good of those who love Him, who
have been called according to His purpose."
- Romans 8:28

It's my favorite verse in the Bible, and I'm so glad it's one of Allan's favorites too.

Unfortunately, Romans 8:28 is one of the most misinterpreted and misunderstood verses in the Bible. So, let's take a few moments to understand what it *does* and *doesn't* say. Let's start with what the verse doesn't say:

It doesn't say that God *causes* all things to happen.

It doesn't say that all things that happen in a Christian's life are "good."

And it doesn't say that God works all things together for *everyone's* good.

Over the course of Allan's adult life, he has run into many people who misunderstand *who* God is and *how* He works. Allan is quick to point out, *God didn't cause my arachnoiditis, but He is using it for His glory.* He also likes to highlight the fact that his spinal cord disease isn't "good," but that hasn't stopped God from using it *for* the good. Finally, Allan points out that God doesn't work all things together for the good of anyone and everyone. God's promise to work all things together for good only applies to His followers—to Christians who love Jesus Christ and have responded to His call to carry out His marching orders (i.e., "His purpose") here on earth.

Consider these thought-provoking paraphrases of Romans 8:28:

> "And we know that all that happens to us is working for our good if we love God and are fitting into His plans."
> (The Living Bible)

> "We can be sure that every detail in our lives of love for God is worked into something good."
> (The Message)

> "We are confident that God is able to orchestrate everything to work toward something good *and beautiful* when we love Him and accept His invitation to live according to His plan."
> (The Voice)

Romans 8:28 goes hand in hand with yesterday's Bible verse: Romans 8:18. Every bit of pain, suffering and rejection we endure for Jesus Christ here on earth will pay handsomely in heaven. Why is that? Because God is working all things together for the good of those who love Him and are helping Christ build His kingdom. God loves those who love Him, and He takes perfect care of those who are doing His life-changing work.

So, take this to heart: According to Romans 8:28, if you love God and are "fitting into His plans," He will work hard for your good. "Every detail of your expressed loved for God" will not go unnoticed. God will "orchestrate everything to work toward something good and beautiful" when you "accept His invitation to live according to His plan."

With that in mind, what are you going to do about it? Are you going to give God a half-hearted love, and hope for the best? Are you going to carry out *some* of God's purposes for your life while ignoring others? Or are you going to love the Lord your God with all your heart, soul, mind and strength and obediently carry out ALL His good plans for you?

Traveling God's good path has never been easy. The world and the prince of this world (Satan) don't make it easy to love and serve Jesus consistently. Loving and serving Jesus is rarely popular, financially profitable or politically correct. But no matter! If we are loving and serving Jesus, God will work all things together for our good. It's a promise!

PRAY WITH ME...

Heavenly Father, You are good and all Your ways are good. Please forgive me for pointing my finger at You when bad things have happened in my life. I have doubted and insulted Your good character. But Your perfect and holy Word has helped me come to my senses. I now realize that, although You have *allowed* them, You haven't *caused* bad things to happen in my life. Because I love and serve You, I believe You are hard at work for my good. You are wading into the ash heap of my pain, suffering and failure, and You are miraculously shaping the ashes into something good and useful. God, only You could do something THAT amazing. So, help me do *my* part: to love and obey You today. And I will trust You to do *Your* part—to work all things together for my good. In Jesus' name, Amen.

NOTES:
thoughts, reflections & action points

DAY 8: CELEBRATE YOUR WEAKNESSES

"But He said to me, 'My grace is sufficient for you, for My power is made perfect in weakness.' Therefore, I will boast all the more gladly about my weaknesses, so that Christ's power may rest on me. That is why, for Christ's sake, I delight in weaknesses, in insults, in hardships, in persecutions, in difficulties. For when I am weak, then I am strong."
- 2 Corinthians 12:9-10

It's one of the great paradoxes of Scripture: I'm at my strongest when I'm at my weakest.

Let me ask you: What is the best way to enjoy a tall glass of ice-cold lemonade on a hot summer day ... in an *empty* glass or in a glass that's already half-filled with something else? Obviously, you'd want it poured into an empty glass, right? Who wants their fresh squeezed lemonade poured into half a glass of tomato juice or into four ounces of day-old coffee? Not me!

Yet when it comes to our spiritual lives, in our arrogance we somehow think we can be at our strongest as Christians when we are leaning on our *own* strength with a little bit of God poured on top. But the Apostle Paul reveals in 2 Corinthians 12 that the opposite is true. We are at our strongest when we are leaning completely on God's *superior* strength, not on our own *inferior* strength. Think of it this way: Your *worst* game of basketball will suddenly become your *best* game if Steph Curry joins your team. And your three strikeouts and two unforced errors won't matter much if Mike Trout joins your baseball team's roster. You see, true greatness more than compensates for your weakness.

In the preceding two verses (2 Corinthians 12:7-8), Paul mentions that he was plagued by "a thorn in my flesh, a messenger of Satan to torment me." Since Paul doesn't give us the specific details, Bible scholars have speculated as to what his "thorn" was. Bad eyesight? Malaria? A speech impediment? A critic who kept hounding him? Guilt over his murderous past? There's no way to know for sure. But whatever Paul's thorn was, it was irritating and weakening him. So, he pleaded with God three times to take it away from him—in much the same way that Allan pleaded with God multiple times to take away his arachnoiditis.

But despite Paul's pleading (and Allan's pleading), God said, *No!* "My grace is sufficient for you, for My power is made perfect in weakness." Let this truth sink deeply into your mind and heart as you consider a few different translations/paraphrases:

> "My grace is enough; it's all you need. My strength comes into its own in your weakness."
> (The Message)

> "My grace is all you need. My power works best in weakness."
> (New Living Translation)

"No. But I am with you; that is all you need. My power shows up best in weak people."
(The Living Bible)

I especially like the way The Living Bible puts it: "My power shows up best in weak people." How true is that! Think about stuttering Moses standing before the mighty Pharaoh. Consider scaredy-cat Gideon blowing his trumpet and smashing his pitcher against an enemy army of over 100,000. And how about the scrawny teenager David facing a fully-armed, nine-foot giant? The list goes on and on. God's power shows up best in weak people. Please say it aloud with me: God's power ... shows up best ... in weak people.

Including you. Paul came to a point in his life where he realized that his thorn wasn't a curse; it was actually a blessing—a gift of grace for which he should be thankful. And God is patiently leading both Allan and you to that same place of resting in His sufficient grace. He is leading you to the place where you can celebrate your bad health, your crummy finances, your broken relationships and your nagging critics. Why? Because they drain you and make you weak. And when you are drained and weak, there's more room for God's grace and strength to fill your cup.

PRAY WITH ME...

Heavenly Father, I really have a hard time wrapping my mind around this one. All my life I've tried so hard to highlight my strengths and hide my weaknesses. I don't *like* feeling insulted, inadequate or weak. But I now realize that my weakness provides the greatest opportunity for You to work in my life. I will always be at my strongest when I, in my weakness, am leaning on Your grace and strength. I believe Your grace is sufficient for me. So, please help me to celebrate my weaknesses and surrender them ALL to You. Use them however You see fit: my weaknesses, my insults, my hardships, my persecutions and my difficulties. For when I am weak, then I am strong. In Jesus' name, Amen.

NOTES:
thoughts, reflections & action points

DAY 9: FIND YOUR STRENGTH IN ME

"I can do everything through Him who gives me strength."
- Philippians 4:13

Like Romans 8:28, it's one of the most loved yet most misquoted verses in the Bible.

Far too many Christians take it out of context, misquote it and end up stumbling down a rabbit trail of discouragement and disappointment with God. So, let's start by noticing what the verse *doesn't* say:

It doesn't say, "I can do everything—PERIOD."

It doesn't say, "*I* get to call the shots—telling God when and where to give me strength."

Now, notice what the verse *does* say:

Christ is the source of your strength ... not you.

"All things" only refers to that which is done "through Christ."

So, the truth is: The promise of Philippians 4:13 is conditional. God will only give you strength to do "all things" if Christ is living *in* you and strengthening you from the inside out. And God will only strengthen you if you are carrying out *His* marching orders. When you are following Christ well, you can be as bold as a lion. In the center of His will, you "can do all things through Christ who strengthens you." But if you are moving and working *outside* His will, all bets are off. Despite how much you *need* God's strength, you won't get it. God has no desire to strengthen you in your rebellion or to buttress you in your sin.

Consider these two biblical paraphrases that will help you wrap your mind around the conditional nature of the Philippians 4:13 promise:

> "I can do all things [which He has called me to do] through Him who strengthens and empowers me [to fulfill His purpose]."
> (Amplified Bible)

> "For I can do everything God asks me to with the help of Christ who gives me the strength and power.
> (The Living Bible)

So, will God give you the strength you need to do this, that or the other? Yes ... *if* you are doing the things God has called you to do. And will God give you the power to do more than you could ever accomplish in your own strength? Yes, *if* you are doing what God has asked of you. Perhaps you've heard the oft-quoted adage, "Where God guides, He provides." In Philippians 4:13, Paul personalizes this truth. *Wherever God leads me and whatever God calls me to do, God makes sure I have all the resources I need to carry out His marching orders successfully—including the strength I need for every task at hand.*

So often Allan has drawn strength from this encouraging verse at times when God has called him to plan and lead a conference, preach a sermon or babysit his two small kids. Conventional wisdom would lead us to believe Allan was *too* weak and in *too much* pain and discomfort to carry out even one of these tasks. But every time God has called him to do something *too big* or *too difficult* in service to Christ, He has supplied Allan with the perfect measure of strength and stamina to accomplish the task. Without fail.

What God did for the Apostle Paul, He *can* do for you. What God has done for Allan, He *will* do for you ... *if* you are a follower of Jesus Christ who is doing what He has called you to do. God never wastes marching orders. If He's called you to do it, He will give you the strength to do it with excellence. So, if you're doing *your* part (obeying Christ), you can be confident that God will do *His* part (strengthening you to do all things).

PRAY WITH ME...

Heavenly Father, I confess: At times I've leveraged this verse to my own advantage. I've taken this Christ-centered verse and made it a me-centered verse. Instead of asking You to strengthen me as I do *Your* work, I've asked You to strengthen me as I do *my* work. Please forgive me. I am not in charge of my life. You are. You are not my butler, genie or Santa Claus in heaven. You are my Father, Master and Commander in Chief in heaven. Please reveal my marching orders today, and give me the strength to do everything You've asked me to do. I believe I can do everything through Christ who gives me strength. In Jesus' name, Amen.

NOTES:
thoughts, reflections & action points

Day 10: Be Strong and Courageous

"Have I not commanded you? Be strong and courageous.
Do not be terrified; do not be discouraged, for
the Lord your God will be with you wherever you go."
- Joshua 1:9

Joshua 1:9 is Allan's favorite verse: the theme verse of his life.

As the Book of Joshua begins, young Joshua was commissioned by God to fill some pretty big shoes: the shoes of Moses. Basically, Joshua was given the hardest job on earth—leading the nation of Israel into the Promised Land—and he must have felt discouraged, overwhelmed and scared. But ... no matter. He had a God-given job to do, and turning into a scaredy-cat wouldn't get the job done. So, the Lord drew Joshua's attention to the one overriding truth that would give him the strength and courage he would desperately need for the days ahead: "the Lord your God will be with you wherever He calls you to go."

If God called Joshua to conquer the city of Jericho, God would be with him in Jericho. If God called him to overthrow the city of Ai, God would be with him in Ai. If God called him to face

Caananite armies that outnumbered the army of Israel five to one, God's promise would *still* stand: He would be with Joshua wherever he went. As long as Joshua followed God's marching orders, the LORD promised to give him victory at every turn. And since Joshua's all-powerful God always keeps His promises, there was no good reason for him *not* to be strong and courageous.

Although Allan may never know this side of heaven why God chose *him* to bear the burden of his rare neurological disease, he knows God is with him. As he faces level-10 pain, God is with him. As he faces immobility, God is with him. As he shares Christ's message of hope and perseverance with those who follow Christ *and* with those who don't, God is with him. Allan has personalized God's charge to Joshua, convinced that God is with him just as He was with Joshua. And since God is with Allan, he has no reason to feel discouraged, anxious or fearful. Since God is with him, he has no reason *not* to be strong and courageous. Joshua held on to that truth till his dying day, and Allan plans to do the same.

As this "10 Days to Persevere" devotional draws to a close, I want to underscore how these ten verses can work together in beautiful symmetry to build Christ's perseverance within you:

In Matthew 11:28, Jesus promises you that whenever you are weary and burdened, He offers you rest for your soul.

In Revelation 3:20, Jesus promises you that even if you've pushed Him out of your life, He is standing at your heart's door knocking—patiently waiting for you to invite Him back into the center of your life as your number one priority.

In Luke 10:2, Jesus offers you the chance of a lifetime: the chance to join Him in His most important work of reaping souls for God's kingdom. Truth be told, nothing will inspire you to persevere like seeing God work through you to lead people to hope and salvation in Jesus Christ.

In Jeremiah 29:11, God promises you as His follower that His plans for you are the *best* plans. They are plans to prosper you and not to harm you, plans to give you hope and a future. Isn't that exciting?

In James 1:2-4, God reveals that your trials are not your enemy. They actually help you develop perseverance and spiritual maturity. So, even when your trials are painful, rejoice and persevere!

In Romans 8:18, God promises you that your glorious rewards in heaven will far outweigh your pain and suffering here on earth. There's no comparison.

In Romans 8:28, God promises you that if you love Him and carry out His plans for you, He will ALWAYS be at work for your good.

In 2 Corinthians 12:9-10, God reminds you that He has given you all the grace you need to persevere through your trials. And when you are at your weakest, you can actually be at your strongest as you allow God's perfect strength to work through you.

In Philippians 4:13, God promises you that you can do "everything" He asks you to do with Christ's strength. Nothing will be too hard or difficult for you as you do Christ's work in Christ's strength.

In Joshua 1:9, God promises to always be with you wherever He leads you. Therefore, there's no reason to be stressed or fearful. Because the King of Kings and Lord of Lords is with you, you *can* and *should* be strong and courageous as you go.

PRAY WITH ME...

Heavenly Father, You've taught me so much over these past ten days. You have reminded me of Your goodness, Your grace, Your wisdom, Your strength and Your perfect purpose and plan for my life. I believe You have a purpose for every one of my trials, and I believe You will be with me wherever You lead me to go. Please forgive me for doubting these truths in the past. Because of who You are, I have no reason to give up or to walk in defeat, discouragement or fear. I have no reason *not* to be strong and courageous. I have no reason *not* to persevere. So, help me from this point forward to persevere, like Joshua, through my trials and be strong and courageous for You. Thank You for being with me as I do. In Jesus' name, Amen.

NOTES:
thoughts, reflections & action points

PHOTOS

The Schwartz Family (Joe, Kim, Joey, Allan & Shavaun) at a
family wedding.

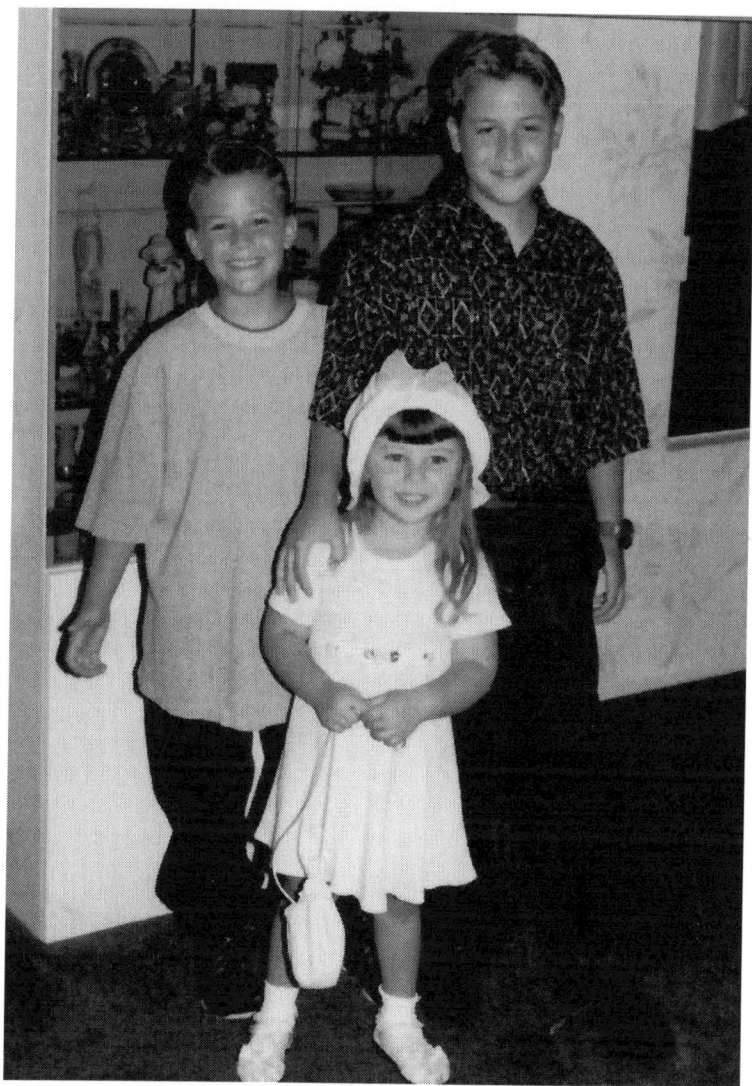

Allan with his big brother Joey and kid sister Shavaun.

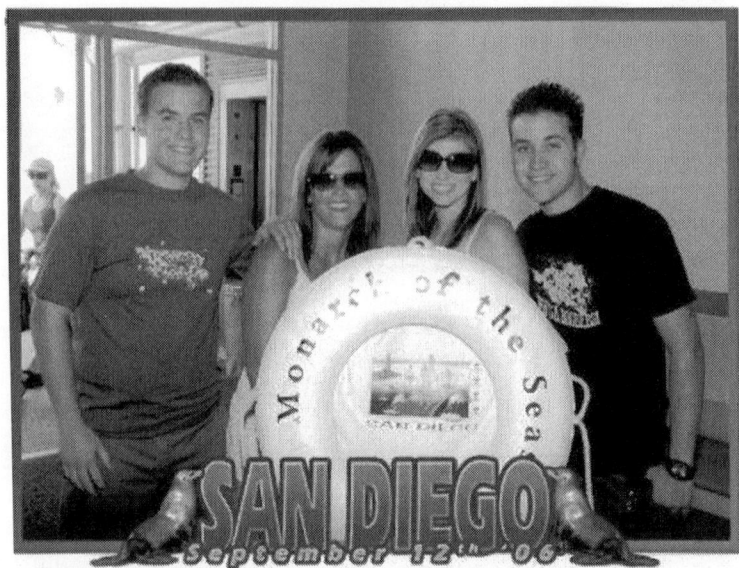

Just six months after having his first major back surgery, Allan
felt healthy enough to join his family for a cruise to Mexico.

Despite the pain, Allan stands to take a picture with his dad,
Tom Carpino and ten Apple Valley fire fighters who helped him
raise the money to get to the Hansa Center.

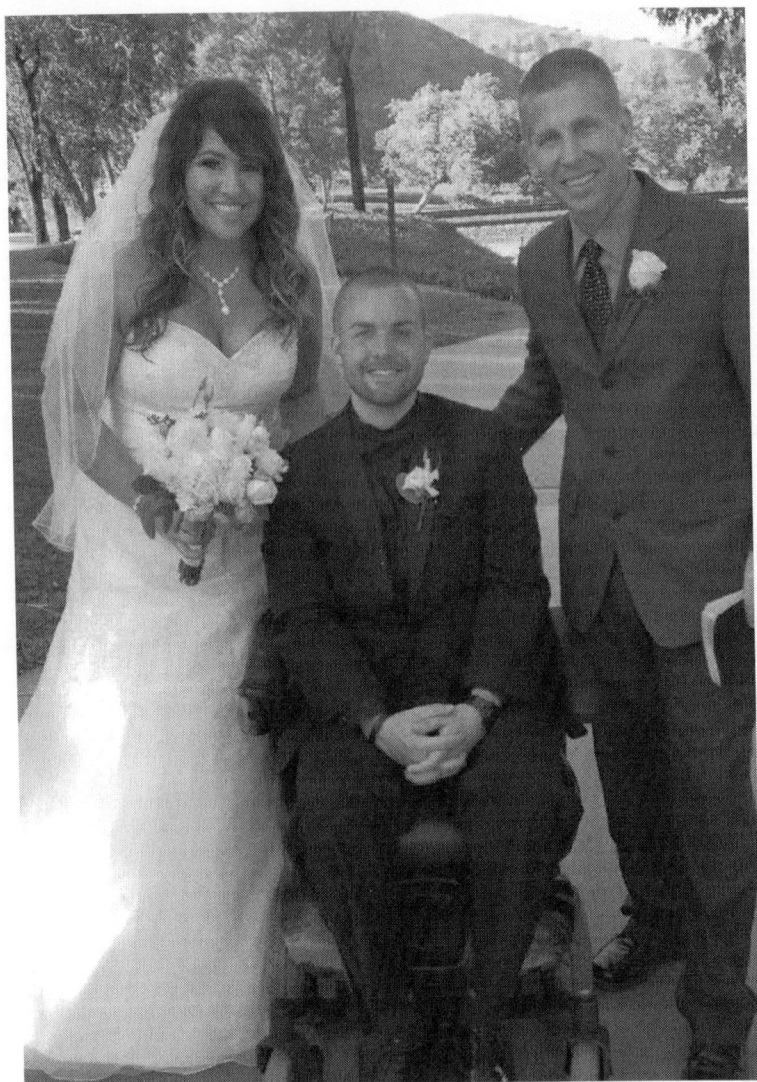

Allan and Brittney on their wedding day with Pastor Dane.

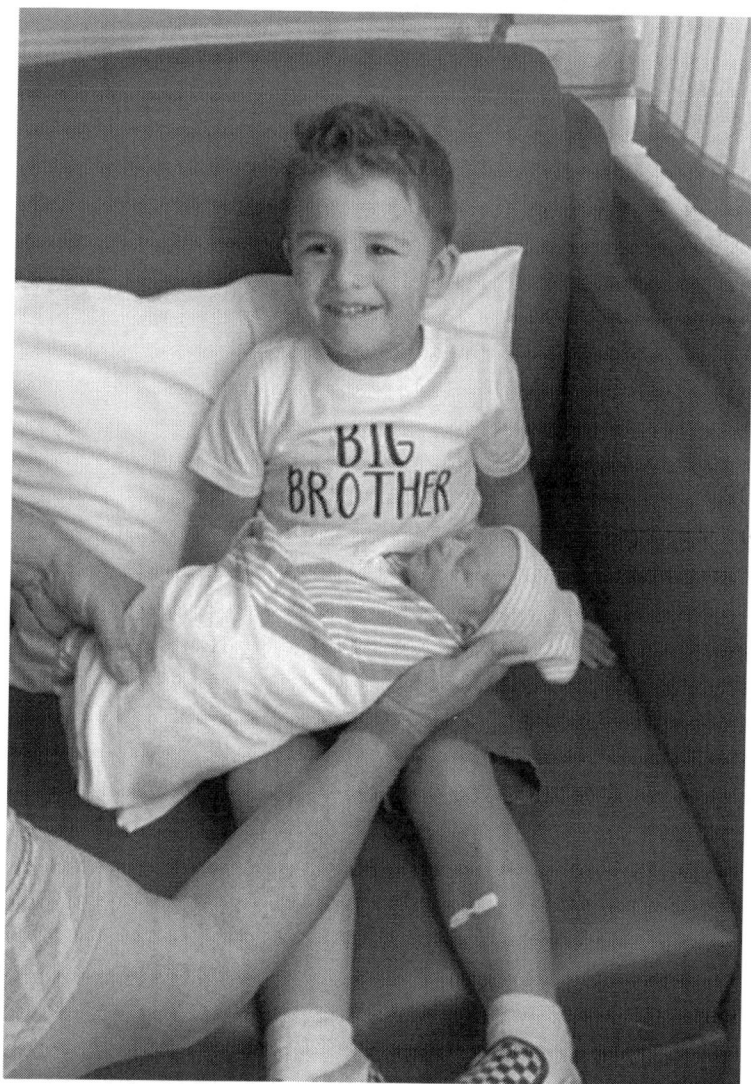

Rylen holds his baby sister Tenley for the first time.

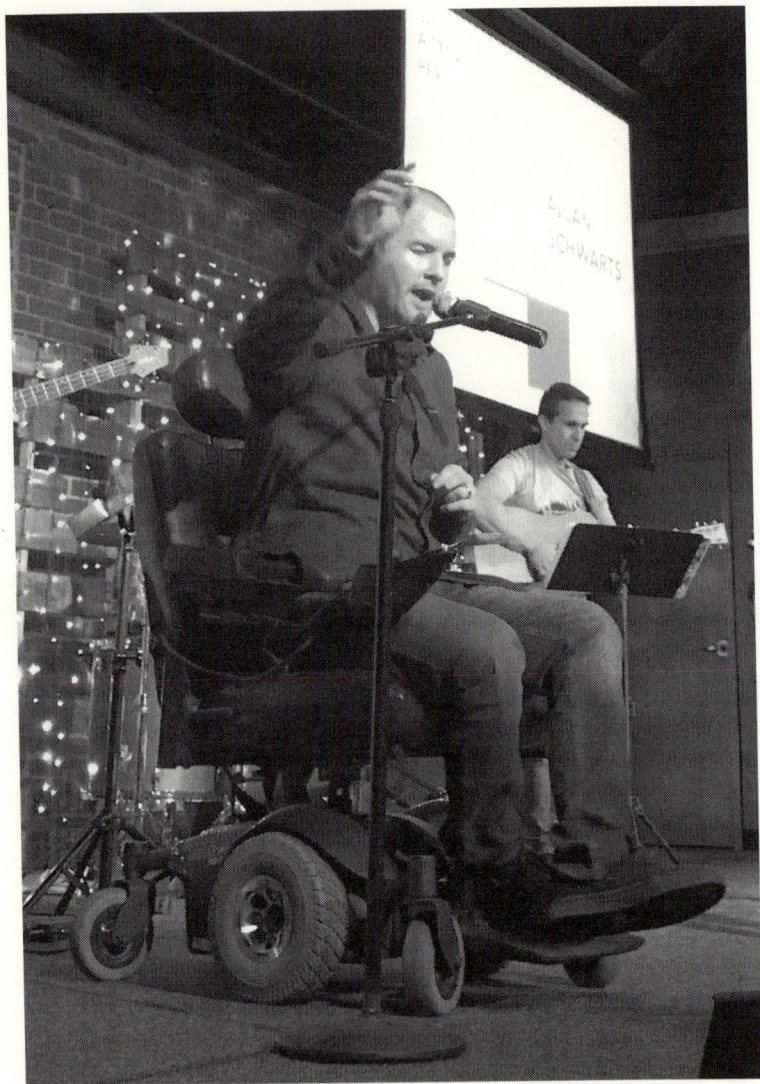

Allan guest speaking at a SoCal church.

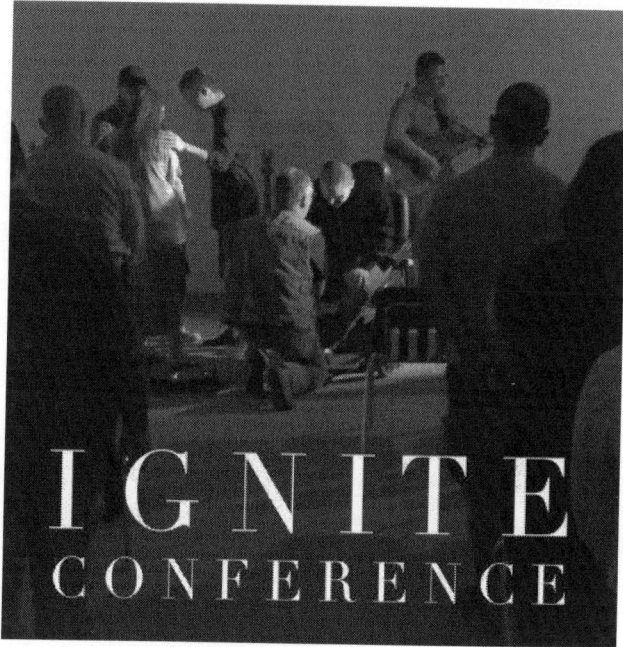

Allan's first conference in Apple Valley, CA.

PERSEVERANCE CONFERENCE

2016

MOTIVATIONAL SPEAKERS
WHO BRING ENCOURAGMENT
AND INSPIRATION

FEATURING ALLAN SCHWARTZ

Diagnosed as the youngest person ever to suffer from an incurable spinal cord disease called Arachnoiditis. This disease has confined Allan to a power chair.

LEARN HOW TO OVERCOME TRIALS AND TRIBULATIONS
AND KNOW THAT NO MATTER WHAT IS THROWN YOUR
WAY THAT GOD IS THERE TO PICK YOU UP!

RAFFLE OVER $1000 IN PRIZES!
HOT-AIR BALLOON RIDE
SPORTS MEMORABILIA
GIFT CARDS
CDS, AND T SHIRTS

ALSO APPEARING

INNOVATORS CREW
Hip-Hop Ministry

PASTOR DANE DAVIS
First Christian Church, Victorville

NICOLE SMITH
Christian Radio Host

JOEL RYANS
Singer

MICHAEL BENNETT
Worship Leader

Missio Dei Congregation, Pomona

HUNTER MARIANO
Pianist/Keyboardist/Organist

JASON LOVE
Comedian

CHRIS AND KRISTIN
HERNANDEZ
Lost son to a rare birth defect

DAVID WOOD
Comedy and Magic

AMANDA ZARATE
Motivational Speaker

SOPHIA ROSE
ChristFM Concerts

KIM SCHWARTZ
Allan's Mom

OCTOBER 29 10AM-4PM - ADVANCE TICKETS $10 - DOOR TICKETS $20
GROUPS OF 10 OR MORE GET TICKETS FOR $5 EACH PAID IN ADVANCE
THE CALIFORNIA EDUCATION AND PERFORMING ARTS CENTER - 11255 CENTRAL AVE, ONTARIO

The flyer for Allan's first Perseverance Conference.

Allan giving Rylen and Tenley the best piggyback rides.

About the Author

Dane Davis has been serving as the lead pastor of Impact Christian Church since 1999. He loves learning and teaching God's word and seeing lives transformed by it. Dane has been married to his college sweetheart, Christine, for over 20 years. They have four amazing daughters who are growing up way too fast.

Dane enjoys jogging, playing just about any sport, and taking teenagers on short-term mission trips.

His first two books--*Holy Huldah!* and *Buoyed Up*--are available through Amazon and other online retailers.